P9-CRR-304

Yankees
Triviology

Neil Shalin

TRIUMPH
BOOKS

Library of Congress Cataloging-in-Publication Data

Shalin, Neil, 1944–
  Yankees triviology / Neil Shalin.
      p. cm.
  ISBN 978-1-60078-624-2
  1. New York Yankees (Baseball team)—Miscellanea. 2. New York Yankees (Baseball team)—History. I. Title.
  GV875.N4S53 2011
  796.357'64097471—dc23
                              2011027440

This book is available in quantity at special discounts for your group or organization. For further information, contact:

   Triumph Books
   542 South Dearborn Street
   Suite 750
   Chicago, Illinois 60605
   (312) 939-3330
   Fax (312) 663-3557
   www.triumphbooks.com

Printed in U.S.A.
ISBN: 978-1-60078-624-2
Design by Patricia Frey
Photos courtesy of AP Images

Contents

Introduction

Somewhere in the deepest recesses of my memory I know I heard or read that Casey Stengel, although he appreciated and admired his Mantles and Berras and Fords, felt that the supporting players were an equal key to the Yankees' success in the '50s.

There were—and this goes back before my time—always great infielders picking up the hard grounders, making the spectacular double plays, and getting the key hits, and outfielders at the corners who could carry a team for a while and always gave you steady defense. While Reynolds/Raschi/Lopat may have been a single word identifying the big three pitchers who dominated baseball during the Yankees' five titles in a row from 1949 to 1953, and Ford came along to bring the Yankees into the next phase of the dynasty, a team doesn't win that consistently on aces alone.

A look back at that period of Yankees history shows that the Yankees could count on a good year or two from little-remembered hurlers such as Bob Grim, Tommy Byrne, Tom Sturdivant, or Johnny Kucks. Stengel could also go to the bullpen and call upon Joe Page or Johnny Sain or Luis Arroyo to put out a fire or keep the Yankees in the game.

When you examine the careers of Hank Bauer and Gene Woodling you realize they weren't just role players but outstanding all-around athletes who had that one trait that all the best Yankees have had over the years: they knew how to win.

Of the infielders, Phil Rizzuto is in the Hall of Fame, but his teammates such as Jerry Coleman, Billy Martin, Gil McDougald, Bobby Brown, and Billy Johnson are not. This in spite of the fact that they contributed to more pennant races and championships over the years than many who are enshrined. And I'm just using that era as an example of the constant stream of Yankees who were integral to the building of professional sports' one true dynasty.

Every one of the five great Yankees eras (Ruth/Gehrig, DiMaggio, Mantle/Berra/Ford, Munson/Jackson, and Jeter/Rivera) has been graced by numerous players who came back when they were past their peaks for one more taste of glory, or people who called on that something extra to have one moment, one series, or one season that contributed to Yankees history.

So, I salute the Babe and Lou and DiMaggio and Mantle and Yogi and Whitey and Thurman and Reggie and Jeter and Mo, but I also know, as you do, that they had help. Hopefully, the reader will discover an unknown player or get new insights or information into those who are somewhat familiar.

In putting the list of top players together I chose one position for each Yankee. So, for instance, McDougald is listed with the second basemen, where he could easily have been with the shortstops or third basemen.

This is all subjective, so you're bound to disagree with a lot of the choices, but that's okay. That's what makes baseball fun.

I would like to express my appreciation to Mike Shalin, Mike Adams, Bill Seiple, Mary Ann Sain, Jim Bouton, Jim Kaat, Hal Naragon, Moose Skowron, Marty Appel, and the Yankees' Jason Latimer for your help in putting this book together.

One

First Base

The Rankings!
1. Lou Gehrig
2. Don Mattingly
3. Tino Martinez
4. Bill "Moose" Skowron
5. Chris Chambliss
6. Wally Pipp
7. Mark Teixeira
8. Hal Chase
9. Joe Pepitone
10. Jason Giambi

Lou Gehrig is the best first baseman of all time. So he would be at the top of any team's list, even though it's been more than 70 years since he played his last game.

Mattingly—a Hall of Famer in our opinion—is at the top of a formidable group that has Jason Giambi at No. 10 because he was usually a designated hitter but played first base at times during several productive years. Martinez, Pipp, Skowron, and Chambliss weren't quite superstars, but it's safe to say that first base for the Yankees was in pretty good hands with all four.

Teixeira, a relative newcomer to the Bronx, can certainly move up several slots if he continues at his present rate of production for a few more years. And Pepitone was a very good ballplayer who went to the outfield for several years.

Don Mattingly

We give him the Hall of Fame on the Sandy Koufax Law, which states that if a player is dominant enough in his prime years and fulfills the required number of years as an active player, then he belongs.

We're not saying that Mattingly was as dominant a hitter as Koufax was a pitcher, but there was a stretch there in the late '80s (1984–89) when many observers thought he was the best player in the game.

In a six-year period, he batted over .300 every year, made the All-Star Game every year, won five of his nine Gold Gloves, won the batting crown in '84 (.343), the RBI title (145), and the total base title (370), as well as being voted the league's MVP that year. In '86 he had the highest slugging percentage, total bases, and OPS. He finished second in the MVP voting that season. The following year he set a record by hitting six grand slams in one season, and he also tied a major league record by hitting home runs in eight consecutive games (10 home runs during the streak).

A back injury suffered during the '87 season bothered Mattingly for the rest of his career, and his power numbers decreased steadily, though he remained a good contact hitter and continued to be a team leader (he was named captain in 1991). He is also regarded by many experts as one of the greatest fielding first baseman of all time.

At the same time that Mattingly played for the Yankees, the Mets also had a first baseman who was his equal as a fielder, Keith

Hernandez. Since both were good hitters—both had won a batting title and an MVP award—many observers believe that Mattingly and Hernandez belong in the Hall of Fame.

"That was always the battle in New York—who was better," said broadcaster Tim McCarver in Mike Shalin's Mattingly biography *Donnie Baseball.* "Oh, it was unbelievable. They were two guys who were maybe the best fielding first baseman in the history of the game."

While Hernandez may have had a slight edge because he had a better arm, Mattingly was more of a power hitter in his prime.

"You talk about Mattingly's offense," McCarver said. "I remember when I was working with ABC and he had all the home runs in eight straight games. I remember how exciting it was to be around. And he was always such a classy guy, the way he carried himself. I didn't know him at the time, but I was always impressed with the way he carried himself and the way he approached the game. He had a religious concentration on what he was doing and how he went about his job."

The fact that Mattingly didn't make the postseason until his final year is one of the factors that Hall of Fame voters point to for not selecting him.

He came up in 1982, the year after the Yankees lost the World Series to the Dodgers, and he retired after the 1995 season with only that one playoff appearance against the Mariners. The Yankees lost to the Mariners, but Mattingly hit .417 and knocked in six runs.

The back injury forced him into retirement after that season at the age of 34.

The following year the Bronx Bombers, with Tino Martinez playing first base, started their string of five straight pennants, including World Series victories in four of those five years.

Lou Piniella believes the injury that limited Mattingly's career is the only thing keeping him from the Hall of Fame. "Legitimate .300

hitter, legitimate RBI guy, legitimate home run–hitting, Gold Glove–type first baseman," Piniella said. "You take away the back injury from Donnie and you have a guy that, say, plays another five or six years in top shape—Hall of Fame numbers."

Bill "Moose" Skowron

Bill "Moose" Skowron was in a nostalgic mood when I spoke to him in March 2011. He had recently gone to New York for an autograph and memorabilia show and spent his time hanging around with former Yankees teammates Yogi Berra, Whitey Ford, Bob Turley, Jim Coates, Art Ditmar, and Hector Lopez. It got him thinking about the good old days.

Skowron, a six-time All-Star, played in the World Series eight times in his career, taking home five championship rings.

Along with Yankees teammates Roger Maris and Mickey Mantle, he still holds the record for most home runs hit in a single season by three teammates. In 1961 the three combined for 143 dingers. Maris, of course, broke Babe Ruth's record with 61 that year, while Mantle finished second in the home run race with 54, and Moose belted 28.

Moose remembered that as a high school player in Chicago in 1946 he went to New York as a member of a *Chicago Herald American* all-star team for a tournament. There he played against future All-Stars Dick Groat, Bob Grim (a New Yorker who would become a teammate on the Yankees), and the great Harry Agganis (who would go on to play first base for the Red Sox before tragically dying at the age of 25).

Skowron was 16 years old when he hit an inside-the-park home run into the gap in right field at the Polo Grounds. "The thing that was so special about the trip was that I got to meet Babe Ruth," said Skowron. "It never occurred to me to ask him for an autograph."

During his early years in baseball, Skowron, who now works for his hometown Chicago White Sox in community relations, met many old-time greats including Ty Cobb and Tris Speaker. When he signed his first Yankees contract, Moose was sent to a winter league where he played for Rogers Hornsby.

"I could kick myself for not getting all those guys to sign a baseball or a program," said Skowron. "So many of them came back for Old-Timers Days at the Stadium."

In 1957, Moose was invited by teammates to the infamous birthday party for Billy Martin at the Copacabana, but he didn't attend. So Skowron wasn't present on the night of the Copa incident, when teammates Mickey Mantle, Whitey Ford, Hank Bauer, and Johnny Kucks went out to celebrate Billy Martin's birthday and wound up being implicated in a brawl with a group of rowdy revelers who were allegedly shouting racial epithets at entertainer Sammy Davis Jr. during his show.

Where was Skowron?

"I told Hank Bauer and his wife that I'd be happy to stay with their two-year-old daughter," said Moose. "I was at the hotel babysitting. What a guy won't do for a buck."

Skowron said he and Bauer, who died in 2007, became really close friends after their playing days. "Hank was a tough ex-marine and a natural leader," Skowron said. "He wouldn't put up with anyone who didn't work hard and hustle. He counted on that World Series check every year, so he would really come down on someone who slacked off because, as he saw it, the guy was taking money out of Hank's pocket."

When Moose first signed with the Yankees he played shortstop and third base, and they even tried him in the outfield. "I couldn't catch a fly ball," he said. "But Johnny Neun worked with me when they decided to make me a first baseman. I even went to the Fred

Astaire Dancing School two nights a week to work on my footwork. I really think it helped."

And speaking of dancing, Skowron also remembers when he and several teammates appeared on *The Arthur Murray Dance Party* TV show. The players got to dance with professional dancers who were dressed in evening gowns, and there was a competition among three ballplayers for the audience to choose the best dancer. "Whitey Ford was doing a jitterbug with one of the dancers, and she fell and was slightly injured," said Skowron. "We were never invited back again."

The recent death of infielder Gil McDougald saddened Skowron. McDougald was a good friend and former roommate. "I was on first base when Gil hit that line drive that hit Herb Score," said Skowron. "Gil was such a compassionate man that I believe that incident really affected the rest of his career. Of course, Score had already proven at a young age that he was one of the best pitchers in the game."

According to Skowron, McDougald—who was a Yankees starter at all three infield positions during his 10-year Yankees career—is a prime example of the team's solid defense during the dynasty era that went from 1949 to 1964.

"We were famous for hitting all those home runs and we had outstanding pitchers through the years," said Skowron. "But I don't think enough credit has been given to the defensive play we had in both the infield and the outfield. Jerry Coleman, Andy Carey, Phil Rizzuto, Bobby Richardson, Billy Martin, Clete Boyer, Tony Kubek, and Eddie Robinson in the infield, and outfielders like Gene Woodling and Hank Bauer were essential to the Yankees winning every year."

Skowron is thrilled to still be around the game at the age of 80, and he's had a great experience working for his hometown White Sox these past 11 years. "Jerry Reinsdorf is an old Brooklyn Dodgers fan," he said. "So there's still that connection to the era that I played for the Yankees. But the White Sox have been great to me. And it's terrific to be at all the home games and meeting the fans at the ballpark and at special events."

Wally Pipp

We know, we know. Wally Pipp was the Yankees first baseman who missed a game in 1925 because of a headache, allowing Lou Gehrig to step in and play the next 2,130 games over 15 years.

As the years went by, "pulling a Wally Pipp" has grown to include anyone who loses their job by taking a day off at an inopportune time, giving a replacement the opportunity to make you irrelevant. Even Pipp added to the mythology years later when he said, "I took the two most expensive aspirins in history."

Now, let's get to the rest of the story.

First of all, it probably wasn't true that Pipp sat out the game because of a headache, which was supposedly the result of a beaning in batting practice the day before. Actually, that beaning took place about a month after Gehrig took over at first base.

Pipp was probably taken out of the lineup along with several other starters in order to shake things up for a Yankees team that wasn't doing well, one that would eventually finish seventh in the American League. And while the story reduces the memory of Wally Pipp to some kind of slacker, a look at his record shows that he was one of the team's best players, a respected slugger who was adept at fielding his position.

Pipp was the Yankees' starting first baseman for 11 years, including their first two pennant winners and the 1923 World Series championship. In fact, his fine career continued with the Reds after it became clear that Gehrig was in the position to stay.

He was a good fielder who was a starter and a slugger in an early Murderers Row–type Yankees lineup that included Babe Ruth, Bob Meusel, and "Home Run" Baker.

For his career, Pipp was a .281 hitter who drove in more than 100 runs in 1923 and '24 and 90 or better four other times. He was the AL home run king in 1915 and 1917 with 12 and nine respectively, before the Babe took the home run to heretofore unseen heights.

Lou Gehrig is embraced by Babe Ruth as "Lou Gehrig Day" is held at Yankee Stadium on July 4, 1939.

1. Whose record did Mattingly tie when he hit home runs in eight consecutive games in 1987?
2. Who later tied the record by also hitting home runs in eight consecutive games?
3. Which first baseman played in seven World Series for the Yankees, all in the 1950s?
4. Which first baseman played in seven World Series for the Yankees in a period spanning the 1950s and '60s?
5. Who was the Yankees starting first baseman after Lou Gehrig retired?
6. Which first baseman hit the walk-off home run for the Yankees in Game 5 of the 1976 ALCS against Kansas City, sending the Yankees to the World Series for the first time since 1964?
7. Which All-Star National League first baseman—who never played for the Yankees—served as their TV and radio announcer from 1971 to 1988?
    a. Ted Kluszewski
    b. Joe Adcock
    c. Bill White
    d. Bill Terry
8. Lou Gehrig attended which Ivy League university?
9. Which Yankees first baseman/outfielder in the 1950s also played pro basketball in the 1940s?
10. Which Yankees first baseman from the 1940s was known for his sweet tenor voice, earning him the nickname "the Bronx Thrush?"
    a. Enrico Pallazzo
    b. Dennis Day
    c. George McQuinn
    d. Buddy Hassett

Answers

1. Dale Long of the Pirates, who later played for the Yankees.
2. Ken Griffey Jr.
3. Joe Collins
4. Bill Skowron
5. Babe Dahlgren
6. Chris Chambliss
7. c. Bill White
8. Columbia
9. Irv Noren
10. d. Buddy Hassett

Two

Second Base

The Rankings!

1. Tony Lazzeri
2. Joe Gordon
3. Willie Randolph
4. Bobby Richardson
5. Robinson Cano
6. Gil McDougald
7. Billy Martin
8. Chuck Knoblauch
9. Aaron Ward
10. Jerry Coleman
11. Steve Sax
12. George "Snuffy" Stirnweiss
13. Alfonso Soriano
14. Horace Clarke
15. Jimmy Williams

Down through the years second base has been one of the Yankees' strongest positions. It has been so good that we made the list a Top 15 in order to include everyone who deserved recognition.

We've got a pair of Hall of Famers in Lazzeri and the recently elected Gordon—who was long overdue—at the top of our list. After that are a pair of great second-sackers, Randolph and Richardson,

Chuck Knoblauch pumps his fist after hitting a game-tying, eighth-inning home run off of Tom Glavine in Game 3 of the 1999 World Series.

who were All-Stars and among the best of their eras. Cano, still a relatively young man, could rank higher in a few years if he keeps up his current pace. McDougald is sixth because we decided to put him at second, even though he could have made the list at either shortstop or third base. The next four were important members of great Yankees teams, while the last five all had more than a moment in the sun.

It's safe to say that the Yankees have been well-covered at second base for just about a century.

Robinson Cano

Is it too early to be talking about Robinson Cano as an eventual Hall of Famer?

Nah.

He's only been in the majors for seven years, but he's already made the kind of impact that ranks him among the best at the position and, if he continues the trend of the past few years, could put him up among the great Yankees of all time.

He ranks behind only Joe DiMaggio in most career hits in his first six years as a Yankee. The Yankee Clipper had 1,183 to Cano's 1,107, ahead of both Don Mattingly and Derek Jeter.

Cano is a native of the Dominican Republic whose dad, Jose, pitched briefly for the Astros in 1989. Robby's been good since he came to the majors in 2005, but in the past three years he's become one of the elite players in the game.

He was the runner-up to A's reliever Houston Street for the Rookie of the Year in '05, hitting .297 with 14 homers and 62 RBIs. He made the All-Star team in 2006, finishing the year with a .342 average, third best in the league. His power numbers went up in '07 as he hit 19 homers and drove in 97 runs. The following year, Cano's production was down, but he put it all together in 2009, when he was one of the team's leaders in the push to the Yankees' first World Series title since 2000. His breakout year in 2009 firmly established him as the No. 5 man in the batting order and maybe the most dangerous hitter on that championship team. Cano hit .320 with 25 home runs and 85 RBIs. He ranked in the top 10 in the AL in hits, extra-base hits, total bases, at-bats, doubles, batting average, runs scored, and triples. He and Derek Jeter became the first double-play combination to both have 200 or more hits in one season.

In 2010, Cano once again made the All-Star team and batted .319, increasing his home-run total to 29 and his RBI total to 109. He also became a more selective hitter, drawing 57 walks, way ahead of his previous best.

"He had a few more home runs this year, but it's really nothing new," Derek Jeter told Chad Jennings of the LoHud Yankees Blog in 2010. "He's just getting more attention now."

Cano won both the Silver Slugger and the Gold Glove and finished third in the MVP voting.

The second baseman's success didn't surprise his teammates.

"The minute that I saw him, I knew he had tremendous potential to be a great big-league player," Mariano Rivera said to Mark Feinsand of the *New York Daily News.* "The way he fielded, the way he hit, it was all so nice and fluid....I don't think we've seen everything from him yet. He's still learning and growing up, so I don't think his game has reached its potential."

Former manager Joe Torre called Cano a cross between Roberto Alomar and Rod Carew.

Cano could be on track to be the Yankees' greatest second baseman ever, and that's really saying something.

Gil McDougald

He hit .300 three times in a 10-year career spent entirely with the Yankees. He never hit more than 14 home runs in a season and he had a career high of 84 RBIs. However, Gil McDougald, who died in November 2010, was one of the most important players on those Yankees teams that dominated baseball from the year he made his first appearance in 1951 to 1960 when he hung up his spikes at the age of 32. He contributed to five Yankees World Series titles and eight pennants. And, during that period, McDougald made—and started—the All-Star game at three different positions: third base, second base, and shortstop.

"He was a great guy to have playing behind you," said his teammate Whitey Ford. "He played all of those positions and played them well."

McDougald began his major league career the same year as Mickey Mantle, and while the slugging switch-hitter struggled and was sent back to the minors for a spell, McDougald flourished as the Yankees' third baseman. He was named the 1951 AL Rookie of the Year, finishing the season with 14 home runs, 72 runs, 63 RBIs, a batting average of .306, and a .396 OBP.

Early in his career, McDougald was known for his unique batting stance, which was considered one of the most unusual in baseball history. It was an open stance with his feet far apart, and he dangled the bat away from his shoulder with the head of the bat below the plane of his hands. Later, when McDougald went into a prolonged slump, Casey Stengel ordered him to switch to a more conventional stance.

In his eventful rookie year, McDougald had six RBIs in one inning, tying a major league record, and he was the first rookie to hit a grand slam in the World Series, which he did at the Polo Grounds in Game 5.

He hit two home runs in the 1953 Series and was a star in the 1958 World Series, hitting two home runs that were instrumental in a pair of Yankees wins.

McDougald started as a third baseman but shifted to second in 1954. Then he replaced shortstop Phil Rizzuto, who retired in 1956.

"He was great at any position we needed him," said first baseman Bill Skowron. "He had good range as a fielder; a strong, accurate arm; and he could hit."

McDougald's pinch-hit single won the 1958 All-Star game for the AL.

As a member of eight Yankees pennant winners, McDougald is among the all-time leaders with 53 World Series games played and 190 at-bats. He hit seven World Series home runs, scored 23 runs, and drove in 24.

The Biographical Encyclopedia of Baseball quoted McDougald as saying that playing defense gave him the greatest satisfaction. "Defense was fun," McDougald said. "My greatest thrill in baseball was when a pitcher came up to me and told me I'd made a helluva play."

He retired after the 1960 season rather than continue his career with an expansion team. He would go on to coach baseball at Fordham.

Despite all of his accomplishments in baseball, though, McDougald is best remembered for hitting the line drive that struck Indians pitcher Herb Score in the face in 1957. Though Score would return to the mound in 1958 and play parts of five more seasons, he would never regain the form of his first two seasons, when he led the league in strikeouts twice and looked like a good bet to be an eventual Hall of Famer. The incident made McDougald sick, and he told reporters that he would quit the game if Score "loses the sight in his eye."

The following year, McDougald was the victim of a line drive himself when he was struck in the head by a ball off the bat of Kansas City's Bob Cerv during batting practice in 1958.

The impact led to progressive hearing loss for McDougald. By the 1980s he had become almost totally deaf and he made very few public appearances.

Ira Berkow wrote an article about him in the *New York Times* in 1994, and physicians who read the article told McDougald about a surgical procedure called a cochlear implant that converts sound to electronic signals. He underwent the implant later that year, and in a few months his hearing was restored.

In his later years, McDougald worked to raise awareness about technology to help the hearing impaired. He was quoted in a *Sports Illustrated* article in 1996: "When you see the progress, particularly with little children, it's so satisfying. It's like hitting a home run with the bases loaded."

Joe Gordon

Anyone who saw Joe "Flash" Gordon play second base for the Yankees in the late 1930s and '40s rated him as one of the best second basemen of all time.

That's why it was surprising that the baseball writers and veterans committees took so long to select him for the Hall of Fame. It was probably because his career numbers weren't viewed as Hall of Fame caliber.

He was a .268 lifetime hitter, and his RBI and runs-scored totals finished just short of 1,000, thanks to two prime years missed because of World War II.

Gordon was finally chosen by the veterans committee in 2009, long after his death.

Not only was the acrobatic native Californian one of the best second basemen, he was probably one of the greatest athletes to ever play the game. While attending the University of Oregon in the 1930s, Gordon competed in baseball, football, gymnastics, soccer, and the long jump. He credited his agility at second base to his time spent as a varsity gymnast.

He even played the violin in the school orchestra.

As a major leaguer, Gordon was one of the key players on four Yankees world championship teams and added another World Series victory in 1948 after he was traded to the Indians. Gordon edged Ted Williams for the AL MVP in 1942. He was a nine-time All-Star and received MVP votes in eight seasons, finishing in the top 10 five times.

Connie Mack, who had seen just about everybody play until that time, said, "Gordon is a whole infield himself. He is the greatest second baseman. Yes, the greatest of all infielders today."

After Gordon starred in the 1941 World Series, Joe McCarthy said, "I'll say right now that the greatest all-around ballplayer I ever saw—and I don't bar any of them—is Joe Gordon."

Gordon had no weakness in the field. He could go to his left or his right, he could come in on slow grounders, and he covered a lot of outfield territory. It was a thrill to watch him make the pivot at second base and show off that strong throwing arm.

"Gordon is the most acrobatic fielder I have ever played with," said Phil Rizzuto. "The plays he could make off balance, throwing in midair, or off one foot, or lying down. Unbelievable!"

Tommy Henrich, the right fielder on those Yankees championship teams, said it was a pleasure just playing behind Gordon every day and having the opportunity to watch him play.

As a hitter, Gordon was a rarity for a second baseman at that time—he could hit with power.

In his rookie year he hit 25 home runs and drove in 97 runs. He hit 20 or more homers seven times, with a high of 32 in both 1939 and 1940, and he had 80 or more RBIs eight times, four times finishing over 100. His 32 home runs in a season stood as an AL record for second basemen for 64 years. In his MVP year, Gordon hit .322 and had an OBP of .408.

He was also a star in the postseason, hitting .400 in the 1938 World Series and .500 in the 1941 Fall Classic.

Gordon had a down year when he got back from the service in 1946, so the Yankees traded him to the Indians for Allie Reynolds, who would become one of the aces of their pitching staff for eight years. But Gordon had a couple of good years left, and in 1948 he got his fifth world championship as the Indians beat the Boston Braves in the World Series.

And now Joe Gordon has his rightful place in Cooperstown alongside the other great second baseman of the first half of the 20th century: Eddie Collins, Rogers Hornsby, Frankie Frisch, Charlie Gehringer, Tony Lazzeri, and his contemporary, Bobby Doerr.

Quiz!

1. Who was the only man ever named World Series MVP as a member of the losing team?
2. Who was the AL batting champion in 1945 with a .309 average?
3. Name three second basemen on this list who never played for a Yankees championship team.
4. Which one of the second basemen on this list later managed for Cleveland and was traded to Kansas City for their manager, Jimmy Dykes?
5. Who was the runner-up to Gil McDougald in the 1951 AL Rookie of the Year voting?
6. Who is the contemporary of Jackie Robinson who also wore No. 42 when he played for the Yankees?
7. Which four people on this list went on to manage in the major leagues?
8. When Joe Gordon played for the Cleveland Indians, which eventual Hall of Famer was both the shortstop and the manager?
9. Which second baseman from this list was part of Murderers Row in 1927?
10. Who was the second baseman on the first Yankees world championship team in 1923?

Answers

1. Bobby Richardson, in 1960
2. George "Snuffy" Stirnweiss
3. Jimmy Williams, Horace Clarke, Steve Sax
4. Joe Gordon
5. Minnie Minoso
6. Jerry Coleman
7. Billy Martin, Willie Randolph, Jerry Coleman, Joe Gordon
8. Lou Boudreau
9. Tony Lazzeri
10. Aaron Ward

Three

Third Base

The Rankings!
1. Alex Rodriguez
2. Graig Nettles
3. Red Rolfe
4. Frank Baker
5. Clete Boyer
6. Wade Boggs
7. Scott Brosius
8. Joe Dugan
9. Billy Johnson
10. Andy Carey
11. Bobby Brown
12. Joe Sewell

By the time Alex Rodriguez retires, his numbers will be right up there with the all-time greats in most offensive categories. Once the premier shortstop in the league as a member of both the Mariners and Rangers, A-Rod

was a quick study when the Yankees moved him to third base because Derek Jeter owned shortstop.

Someone suggested that in building a major league all-star team consisting of players since World War II, Rodriguez could be the entire left side of the infield as both a shortstop and third baseman. While many admitted that A-Rod's numbers could justify this choice, their preference for the all-time team would be Cal Ripken or Jeter as the shortstop *and* either George Brett and Mike Schmidt at third base.

Others reject the notion completely, pointing to A-Rod's failure to help deliver a championship on his previous clubs and because they feel that he is more focused on himself than the team and has been a distraction, even during some great years with the Yankees.

"I would just not want him as a teammate," said one observer.

There are three Hall of Famers on this list, and all three had their best years before joining the Yankees.

Baker was the third baseman for the A's great $100,000 infield in the early 1910s, Boggs won five AL batting crowns as a member of the Red Sox, and Sewell was the starting shortstop for the Indians throughout the 1920s.

Nettles and Boyer were among the great defensive third basemen of all time and played key roles on 10 Yankees World Series teams between them. While neither hit for a high average, Nettles was one of the league's feared power hitters.

Graig Nettles

"When I was a little boy, I wanted to be a baseball player and join a circus. With the Yankees I've accomplished both."

—Graig Nettles, about playing for the colorful Yankees team that was known as "the Bronx Zoo"

Graig Nettles is one of the best third baseman who is not in the Hall of Fame. He's got the credentials as a supreme fielder and a primetime slugger on winning Yankees teams who took seven trips to the postseason during his 11 years with the club. Five of those playoffs resulted in World Series appearances, and two ended with championship rings.

Nettles finished his career with 390 home runs, winning the home run title with 32 in 1976. His 319 home runs in the American League are the most ever by a third baseman. He had 1,314 RBIs and 2,225 hits, and he saved his biggest performances for the biggest stage.

He was voted MVP of the 1981 ALCS.

He won two Gold Gloves and he holds both the single-season major league record for assists by a third baseman as well as being tied with Brooks Robinson for the second most assists of all time. In fact, Nettles and Robinson have four of the six 400-assist seasons by a third baseman in major league history.

Any talk of Nettles always begins with his incredible fielding exhibition in Game 3 of the 1978 World Series against the Dodgers. The Dodgers won the first two games, but in Game 3 Nettles made four great plays to give the Yankees their first win on their way to a comeback Series win.

In the third inning with the Yankees leading 2–1, a runner on first, and two out, Reggie Smith smashed a shot down the third-base line. Nettles made a diving stop and threw Smith out at first to retire the side. Smith was then robbed by Nettles again in the fifth. With the tying run on second, Nettles knocked down a blistering line drive, keeping the runner from scoring and holding Smith to an infield single. The next hitter was Steve Garvey, and he sent another screaming line drive Nettles' way, but the Yankees' third baseman went down to his knees, backhanded it, and forced Smith at second to end the inning. And finally, in the top of the sixth with the bases loaded and two out, the Dodgers' Davey Lopes hit a hard grounder toward third, where Nettles made a great stop and then a strong throw forcing the runner at second and ending the inning.

The Yankee Stadium crowd gave Nettles a standing ovation as he trotted into the dugout.

"Graig never had to take a backseat to anybody, the way he played defense," said Joe Torre, who said Nettles was a little more acrobatic than Brooks Robinson.

"Graig was one of those real quiet big-game guys," said teammate Willie Randolph. "He wasn't someone who wowed you or stood out, but he was very smooth, very fundamental, and he always seemed to step up in the big game."

Paul Molitor credits Nettles for his mental approach to the game.

"He always knew what the pitcher was throwing," Molitor said. "And it was Nettles who told Gossage that George Brett's bat had too much pine tar and should be checked if he hit a home run, which he did...Nettles always seemed to be in the right place at the right time."

Hawk Harrelson called Nettles one of the best fastball hitters he'd ever seen.

Nettles was also known for his quick and irreverent wit.

In addition to the quote at the beginning of this section referring to the famous "Bronx Zoo" Yankees, Nettles' witticisms included the following:

"In one year Sparky Lyle went from Cy Young to Sayonara."

"The best thing about being a Yankee is getting to watch Reggie Jackson play every day. The worst thing about being a Yankee? Getting to watch Reggie Jackson play every day."

While being acknowledged as one of the best during his era at this position, Nettles hasn't received much support for the Hall of Fame, probably in part because of his less-than-stellar .248 lifetime batting average.

Red Rolfe

Red Rolfe was the Yankees' third baseman for almost a decade and was considered the best at his position—as both a hitter and a fielder—in the time that he played.

In the nine years that Rolfe started at third base for the Yankees, the team went to the World Series six times, winning five titles.

And it wasn't as though Rolfe was just a supporting player. He batted leadoff or second on a team that dominated baseball in the late 1930s and early '40s. He set the table and was often on base when DiMaggio, Gehrig, Henrich, Keller, and Dickey came to the plate.

Rolfe could hit to all fields, work out a walk (he had a .360 OBP), and hit behind the runner. He was the classic cerebral ballplayer who did all the little things that help a team win over the long haul. He was good for more than 100 runs scored a season, had a .289 lifetime average, made the All-Star team four times, and led the league in fielding twice.

"In the field he had the dead-sure hands of Pie Traynor," wrote Ed Rumill in *Baseball Magazine* in 1949.   "A stronger arm and just as good as Pie on slow hit balls or bunts down his way." Rumill pointed out that Rolfe's greatness as a ballplayer went far beyond his ability at the plate or around the bag. "He stood out as a hustler and possessed the brain of a natural-born big leaguer. Red was a money ballplayer. He always managed to produce that extra something when the chips were piled in front of him."

In 1950, as the manager of the Tigers, Rolfe almost guided his team to the AL pennant, falling just three games short of the Yankees.

Rolfe's best year was 1939, when he hit .329, led the league in hits with 213, runs scored with 139, and doubles with 46, all in a season when the Yankees won the pennant by 17 games and swept the Reds in the World Series. Rolfe also hit 14 home runs and knocked in 80 runs that year.

In the six World Series in which he played, Rolfe had a lifetime .284 batting average, hitting .400 in the 1937 Series.

In a 1969 poll, Rolfe was named the Yankees' best third baseman of all time.

"Red was one of my favorite players when I was a kid," said Dr. Bobby Brown, the former Yankees third baseman "He was a great fielder, could run like the devil, and could hit for a high average. He hit to all fields. And he played his entire career with ulcerative colitis, and there was no treatment for [it] in those days."

The illness certainly shortened Rolfe's playing career, his managerial career, and ultimately, his life. Rolfe, a Dartmouth graduate, returned to his alma mater as both a baseball coach and the athletic director. He died at the age of 60.

1. Who hit home runs off Hall of Famers Christy Mathewson and Rube Marquard in the 1912 World Series, when he was a member of the Philadelphia Athletics?

2. Name the Yankees third baseman who went on to become the president of the American League.

3. Which Yankees third baseman was known for his superstitions? For instance, he ate chicken before every game.

4. Which Yankees third baseman was the brother of a major league third baseman who was named the NL MVP in 1964?

5. Who is the Yankees third baseman who struck out only 114 times in a Hall of Fame major league career of more than 7,000 at-bats?

6. Name the person on this list who spent most of his career as a shortstop on the Cleveland Indians.

7. Which Yankees third baseman's younger brother was an All-Star major league catcher and later managed in the big leagues?
8. True or False? Clete Boyer won three Gold Gloves as the starting third baseman for the Yankees.
9. Name the third baseman who served as Yankees team captain from 1982 to 1984.
10. Which Yankees third baseman became a cardiologist when his playing days were finished?

Answers

1. Frank "Home Run" Baker, who earned his nickname as a result of that feat
2. Bobby Brown
3. Wade Boggs
4. Clete Boyer
5. Joe Sewell
6. Joe Sewell
7. Joe Sewell
8. False, he never won a Gold Glove as a member of the Yankees. In the years he started at third base in New York (1960–66) Brooks Robinson of the Orioles won the Gold Glove every year. Boyer won his only GG as a member of the Atlanta Braves in 1970.
9. Graig Nettles
10. Bobby Brown

BONUS Quiz!

As of this writing, A-Rod is in his eighth season as a Yankee, he has already won two (of his three total) MVP awards in the Bronx, and he's moved up among the Yankees' all-time leaders in a number of categories. He's seventh in home runs and 13th in RBIs. But he's not yet on the list of Yankees who have a thousand RBIs in pinstripes. Can you name the 12 players who have at least 1,000 RBIs in their Yankees careers? (Hint: seven are in the Hall of Fame.)

Answer

Lou Gehrig (1,995), Babe Ruth (1,971), Joe DiMaggio (1,537), Mickey Mantle (1,509), Yogi Berra (1,430), Bernie Williams (1,430), Bill Dickey (1,209), Tony Lazzeri (1,154), Derek Jeter (1,151), Don Mattingly (1,099), Jorge Posada (1,038), and Bob Meusel (1,005).

Four

Shortstop

The Rankings!
1. Derek Jeter
2. Phil Rizzuto
3. Tony Kubek
4. Frank Crosetti
5. Everett Scott
6. Roger Peckinpaugh
7. Bucky Dent
8. Kid Elberfeld
9. Mark Koenig
10. Gene Michael

Evidence that shortstop has not been the Yankees'
greatest strength through the years can be found
here as Jeter rises to the top of the list while still an
active player. It's not that the Captain hasn't earned
his spot. He will go down as one of the all-time great
Yankees—a definite Hall of Famer who's sure to see his
No. 2 retired.

Rizzuto, a fan favorite and a beloved broadcaster for generations, was a great fielder, one of the supreme bunters of all time, and the 1950 AL MVP. While Rizzuto wasn't in Jeter's class as an all-around player, the Yankees sure did win a lot with Scooter in the middle of the infield.

After Rizzuto retired, Gil McDougald held the position with his usual effectiveness, and then Kubek made it a team strength for a number of years, before he retired at 30 years old.

Crosetti was a part of 17 World Series titles in an almost four-decade run as a Yankees player and coach, and Scott was the best-fielding shortstop of his time. They were both classic "good-field hardly-hit" shortstops.

Peckinpaugh was not a bad hitter and was even the Yankees captain, but he was inconsistent in the field—and at times, consistently bad. As a member of the Senators he committed a record eight errors in the 1925 World Series. His team lost.

Dent was a pretty good shortstop who stamped his place in Yankees history when he hit that famous home run in the 1978 playoff game against the Red Sox.

Elberfeld was an old-fashioned, blood-and-guts type who played aggressively, a la Ty Cobb. Michael was another good fielder whose influence on Yankees lore was greater as the executive who built the great Jeter-Rivera-Posada-Pettitte teams of recent years.

Derek Jeter

Derek Jeter has done the impossible during his baseball career.

He and his mates on the great teams of the late 1990s and early 2000s actually made a lot of people around the country stop hating the Yankees, which is remarkable because it was done during an impressive run of successful seasons, when non-New Yorkers could have easily increased their animosity. Although we're sure that Boston fans have reserved their right to keep hating.

Gene Michael—who ran the club when George Steinbrenner was banished from the game because of illegal campaign contributions—put together a team of talented, likeable, homegrown athletes who could play and who acted in a friendly, sportsmanlike manner that drew admiration from baseball fans everywhere.

"Homegrown" may be the key word here.

One reason it was so easy to dislike the Yankees has always been the way they flashed their cash in order to build the team. From the purchase of Babe Ruth and many of his colleagues from the champion Red Sox in the late 1910s, to the use of the Kansas City A's as a sort of farm team in the '50s, to George Steinbrenner buying All-Star players such as Catfish Hunter, Reggie Jackson, and Goose Gossage as if they were cut-out dolls to be dressed in Yankees pinstripes in the '70s, the Yankees always fulfilled the general populace's image of the arrogant, superior New Yorkers who viewed the rest of the country as a mere flyover on the way to California.

But Gene Michael changed a lot of that. The Yankees team that emerged as world champions in 1996 (the Yankees' first World Series title since 1978) was just about as homemade as Mrs. Letterman's Thanksgiving pies in Indiana.

They say that you build a champion by making your team strong up the middle. Well, these Yankees were indeed that: starting at home plate with Jorge Posada, to the pitcher's mound where you found lefty and postseason ace Andy Pettitte and closer supreme Mariano Rivera, to the middle infield with Jeter, and to center field, where Bernie Williams presided.

All real Yankees.

Add first baseman Tino Martinez, third baseman Scott Brosius, and outfielder Paul O'Neill, who seemed like native Yankees the minute they put on pinstripes, and you've got a team that any Gotham-hater could love.

Oh, they dropped in a high-priced purchase here and there like Roger Clemens, Wade Boggs, Randy Johnson, and Jason Giambi, and you could surely hate those villainous rent-a-players, but they were, in their way, just supporting players, not the dominant personalities like the homegrowns and the true transplants.

It's hard to find a real baseball fan who can say anything bad about Jeter or Rivera.

The ballclub's image wasn't hurt by the presence of a humble manager like Joe Torre, either. Torre was a former baseball great and a native Brooklynite who just seemed like "a straight dude" and who turned out to be an excellent manager, an admirable father figure, and the face of the franchise all those years.

"I admire those Yankee teams," said baseball historian Mike Adams, who was born in Cincinnati, spent his college years in Boston, and now resides in the Chicago area. "I like both their physical and their mental approach to the game. It wasn't like the cocky Bronx Zoo team. You knew early on that this was a great team taking shape."

Adams sees Torre and his personality as being central to the team's success and the popular support it built nationwide.

"He's a likeable guy, especially compared to others who've run the team," said Adams. "You root for a guy like that to succeed. He came in and he got it. He had command of everything, and the team was a reflection of him."

And since this is the shortstop chapter, we'll focus on Jeter.

"You can make the argument that Jeter is the best shortstop of all time," Adams said, "He has 3,000 hits. He should have been the MVP the year Justin Morneau won. Think of the big hits Jeter's had in the playoffs, the clutch plays in the field. Every time I've seen him play he's had a huge impact on the game, and it's not always measured in stats. He gets what it means to be a Yankee and he embraces that and gets everyone else to buy into it. And he conducts himself like a true professional."

Jeter's profound impact on the team was apparent as soon as he came to the majors.

He started at shortstop on Opening Day 1996, and hit his first major league home run. He helped lead the Yankees to their first World Series championship since 1978 and hit .361 in the playoffs. His season numbers, which include a .314 batting average with 104 runs scored and 78 RBIs, earned him the Rookie of the Year Award.

"You knew from the start there was something special about him," said Torre. "The way he carried himself, the way he played the game. He's just all about winning."

In his second year, Jeter's average dipped to .291, while his other numbers remained about the same, as the Yankees lost to the Indians in the Division Series. In 1998, Jeter really hit his stride

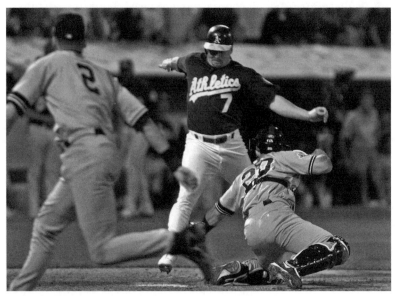

Jeremy Giambi is tagged out at home in the 2001 ALDS after Derek Jeter's famous "flip" to Posada.

with a .324 average, a league-leading 127 runs, 19 home runs, and 84 RBIs as the Yankees won 114 games and swept the Padres in the World Series. That '98 team is inarguably one of the greatest baseball teams of all time.

The Bronx Bombers made it three titles in a row by winning in 1999 and 2000. In 2000, Jeter became the first player ever to win the MVP of both the All-Star Game and the World Series in the same season.

"I'm trying to think who the best Yankee shortstop I've ever seen is, and I keep coming back to this kid," said Hall of Famer Phil Rizzuto, the No. 2 man on our list.

Jeter went to the All-Star Game in every year but one between 1998 and 2010. He was named the Yankees' Player of the Year five times, won the Gold Glove Award five times, and the Silver Slugger Award four times. Jeter was also a two-time winner of the Hank Aaron Award (2006 and 2009), and he won the Roberto Clemente Award (2009), the Sports Illustrated Sportsman of the Year (2009), and the Espy Awards Best MLB Player (2007).

In most years he's among the league leaders in hits, runs scored, and batting average, and he's finished among the top 10 in AL MVP voting seven times.

In 2010, Jeter passed Lou Gehrig for most career hits by a Yankee, and he's high on the list of all-time Yankees leaders in most offensive categories. He's had 200 or more hits seven times. And to complete the statistical picture, Jeter has 236 home runs, 1,719 runs, 1,151 RBIs, 328 stolen bases, almost a thousand walks, a .313 average, and a .383 OBP.

Plus, he's kept up his production at that level in the postseason, while turning in numerous key plays in the field and delivering important hits in clutch situations.

"The guy is baseball in New York," said Twins manager Ron Gardenhire.

Kid Elberfeld

Now we take the way-back machine to the early part of the 20th century, when a colorful character named Norman "Kid" Elberfeld played shortstop for the Highlanders (the name of the Yankees organization from 1903 to 1912).

Elberfeld, who was known as "The Tabasco Kid," because of his hot temper and his fiery style on the field, played the game rough and dirty in the style of the old Baltimore Orioles of the 1890s.

The Kid was always fighting with opposing players and umpires, using abusive language, and sometimes getting physical with the arbiters. One time he threw a clod of mud into an umpire's open mouth. It's believed that he was thrown out of more games than any player of that time.

In Ty Cobb's rookie year Cobb slid head-first into second base and Elberfeld was waiting for him. The Tabasco Kid mashed his knee into the back of Cobb's neck, grinding his face into the dirt. Rough? Sure. But the rookie learned his lesson. Cobb never slid into a base head-first again. Instead he'd come into the base with spikes flying, as was the style back then.

Elberfeld's shins were frequently cut by sliding base runners, and he was known to go into the dugout and clean his wounds with whiskey.

Elberfeld, played for New York from 1903 to 1909, and he had a major league career that lasted 14 years.

He was regarded as one of the best shortstops in the league.

The Kid covered a lot of ground at short, and he was a fair hitter who usually ranked with the league leaders in hit-by-pitches. In fact, he's near the top 10 all time in HBP, with 165.

In 1907 he became the first American League player to steal home twice in the same game.

Elberfeld was the starting shortstop on the Highlanders team that almost won the pennant in 1904, as they were led by pitcher Jack Chesbro's 41 victories, one of those records that will never be broken. Boston (the Americans before they were the Red Sox) won the pennant by a game and a half.

There was no World Series that year because John McGraw, the NL pennant-winning Giants manager, announced that he wouldn't play. This was because it looked like the Highlanders could win and because McGraw was still angry at AL president Ban Johnson for some old disputes over club ownership.

Elberfeld's shortstop range narrowed in his later years when recurring injuries took their toll. Then, when manager Clark Griffith resigned in 1908, Elberfeld took over and managed the team to a last-place finish.

While The Tabasco Kid never managed in the majors again, he did have a long career playing and managing in the minor leagues. Contrary to his image as a major league player, Elberfeld was known as a patient and thoughtful manager.

In his autobiography, Casey Stengel remembered that as a young player he and Elberfeld were teammates, and the old veteran was very supportive. The two became good friends. Stengel was grateful for how generous Elberfeld was with his time, his baseball knowledge, and big-brotherly advice.

In his later years, Elberfeld ran an apple orchard on Signal Mountain, Tennessee, near Chattanooga, and raised a family of five girls and a boy. He lived there until his death at 65 in 1944.

🧢 Quiz!

1. Which Yankees shortstop was hit in the throat by a bad hop and had to leave Game 7 of the 1960 World Series?

2. Which Yankees GM—and former shortstop—is credited with putting together the World Series teams that featured Jeter, Jorge Posada, Bernie Williams, and Mariano Rivera?

3. Who was the shortstop on the Yankees for their first World Series championship in 1923?

4. Which shortstop was a member of 17 Yankees world championship teams as a player and coach?

5. Which of these shortstops—as a member of the Washington Senators— committed eight errors in the 1925 World Series?

6. Who was the AL MVP in 1950?

7. Who led American League shortstops in fielding percentage eight straight years from 1916 to 1923?

8. Who hit a home run against the Red Sox in the 1978 playoff game to determine the American League pennant winner?

9. Who holds the Yankees record for most career hits?

10. Who won three World Series as a member of the Red Sox before he was traded to the Yankees?

Answers

1. Tony Kubek
2. Gene Michael
3. Everett Scott
4. Frank Crosetti
5. Roger Peckinpaugh
6. Phil Rizzuto
7. Everett Scott
8. Bucky Dent
9. Derek Jeter, with more than 3,000.
10. Everett Scott

Five

Left Field

The Rankings!
1. Charlie Keller
2. Bob Meusel
3. Roy White
4. Hideki Matsui
5. Rickey Henderson
6. Gene Woodling
7. Lou Piniella
8. George Selkirk
9. Hector Lopez
10. Tom Tresh

There are no all-time greats here. There are no Hall of Famers except Henderson, and he played a good portion of his career elsewhere. Early in his Yankees career, Keller was putting together numbers that probably would have gotten him to the Hall of Fame, but a bad back started him downhill at 29, when a slugger is usually in his early prime years. White has

been so famous for being underrated through the years that he's in danger of becoming overrated.

It's become a cliché that he was a "quiet leader" of the Yankees during their down years after CBS bought the team in the 1960s. He was a consummate professional who could field and hit and just played good baseball for over a decade. He stuck around long enough to be rewarded for his service by lasting until the team's revival in the 1970s, and he was still a starter when the Yankees played in the World Series in the late 1970s. So White got his ring. In the era of SABR and the reliance on a whole new way of looking at the game statistically, White, who was a two-time All-Star, has achieved new recognition for his efficiency and his ability to get on base and advance runners via walks, sacrifices, and sacrifice flies.

Selkirk was an All-Star, but he played the other outfield positions as well, and Piniella, of course, carried a big bat during the Yankees' Bronx Zoo period in the late 1970s and early '80s.

As we said, this is merely a solid position in Yankees history, but imagine if 1) Keller doesn't get injured and fulfills his great potential, 2) Rickey plays most of his career as a Yankee, 3) Matsui arrives in New York five or six years earlier, and 4) Meusel is magically turned into a hustling player who lives up to his five tools. Put those four at the head of a list that includes solid pros like White, Woodling, and Selkirk, and then you've got something. The Yankees may have even built a dynasty.

Bob Meusel

Bob Meusel was the third bat in Murderers Row, the No. 5 hitter in the lineup behind Ruth and Gehrig. His ability to hit, run, and field, along with his reputation for possessing the greatest outfield arm of his time (1920–29 with the Yankees) makes him one of the most talented players of that era. He was a natural.

Meusel was a key contributor on six pennant-winning teams, including the first three Yankees World Series champions. He still ranks among the team's all-time top 20 in many categories, more than 70 years after he retired. Meusel is seventh in triples (87), eighth in batting average (.309), and tenth in doubles (338), as well as being between 11th and 15th in slugging percentage, RBIs, and total bases, and sitting at 17th in hits and stolen bases. (He led the team in stolen bases five times.)

In 1925, he won two-thirds of the Triple Crown with 33 home runs and 138 RBIs. He hit over .300 seven times, and he's one of only two players in modern times (Babe Herman is the other) to hit for the cycle *three* times.

But, when talking about Meusel the conversation always comes back to his unbelievable arm.

"Nothing pleases him more than to have a hostile base runner gamble with his 'whip' by attempting to score from second on a single or from third on an outfield fly," said sportswriter Fred Lieb, who covered the Yankees.

Lieb claimed he never saw a player with a stronger arm than Meusel.

Twice, early in his career, Meusel led the league in outfield assists, but his number decreased because people were afraid to run on him. Even Ty Cobb stayed at third on flies hit to Meusel.

Yankees manager Miller Huggins said that many runs were prevented just because Meusel was in the outfield. Huggins also praised Meusel's all-around skills, claiming that, with the exception of Babe Ruth, nobody hit the ball harder.

"Bob had everything to make him great," Huggins said. "A good eye at bat; strength; a natural, easy swing; and that wonderful steel arm. But his attitude was one of just plain indifference."

Meusel was probably the most nonchalant player who ever lived. He loped after fly balls and hits, and sometimes didn't run out grounders. His reaction was the same whether he hit a home run or took a called third strike. He was immune to both praise and criticism. The outfielder is quoted in *Baseball Magazine* in 1926: "Hustling is rather overrated in baseball. It's a showy quality that looks well and counts for little."

Meusel wasn't close to many of his teammates. However, he was close friends with Babe Ruth, with whom he spent a lot of time barnstorming and partying after hours. In some cities, Meusel switched positions with Ruth because the Babe hated playing the sun field. In later years, Meusel acted as himself in both of the famous biopics about his former teammates: *The Pride of the Yankees* and *The Babe Ruth Story*.

The Hall of Fame veterans committee has considered him for the Hall of Fame. But the 6'3" slugger never made it to Cooperstown, even though he was one of the most talented players of his time and on the dominant team of the decade.

Gene Woodling

Gene Woodling wasn't known as a home run hitter, but you couldn't prove that to Hall of Famer Early Wynn. In 1951, Woodling hit a home run off Wynn, the Indians pitcher, on the 24th of three consecutive months. The first was on June 24 in New York, when the Yankees left fielder hit a two-run home run in the eighth inning to break a 3–3 tie and give the Yankees a 5–3 win. A month later, on July 24, the Indians came back to New York and Wynn, leading 2–0, faced Woodling in the sixth inning. Gene hit a two-run home run to tie the score and the Yankees went on to win the game 3–2.

And what uniform number did Wynn wear? Twenty-four, of course.

Woodling was a .284 hitter with an OBP of .386. He was usually the first or second batter in those powerful Yankees lineups that won five straight World Series titles from 1949 to 1953. He hit better than .300 five times and walked almost twice as much as he struck out during a 17-year career that started with the Indians and also included stops with the Pirates, Orioles, Senators, and Mets.

Woodling, as evidenced by his home runs against Wynn, was particularly good in the clutch, coming up with the hit that would start a rally or win the game. He also stepped up big-time in the World Series, hitting homes runs in the 1951, '52, and '53 Fall Classics, and he had a lifetime .318 batting average in the Series. He batted .400 in the 1949 World Series and .429 in the sweep of the Phillies in 1950.

"They had nicknamed Tommy Henrich 'Old Reliable,'" Woodling once said. "And, since I came from near him in Ohio, Yankees broadcaster Mel Allen nicknamed me 'Old Faithful.'"

Woodling liked to think that the nickname applied to the way he played the game.

"I had the good fortune to be able to win ballgames with late-inning hits. That was where I excelled and how I made my money."

His home run against Bob Feller of the Indians—again, the Indians—in 1952 gave the Yankees a 1–0 win and preserved one of Allie Reynolds' two no-hitters that year.

Ted Williams and Johnny Sain were among many major league greats who thought the left-handed–hitting Woodling—whose batting stance was to fold up into a deep crouch—was one of the toughest outs in the American League.

When kids in those days played "guess the batting stance," Woodling's was always one of the most popular, along with those of Jackie Robinson, Gil McDougald, Andy Pafko, and Stan Lopata.

Plus, Woodling was an all-around player who could run and throw, and he was regarded as one of the best outfielders of his time. Casey Stengel sometimes platooned Woodling, and even in the outfielder's best year of 1953, he had only 395 at-bats. Though he did lead the American League that year with a .429 on-base percentage.

Roy White

Before we get to the quiz, let's just give you a few more words about Roy White, the quiet professional who was a fine all-around player who did all the little things to help a team.

White had the misfortune of coming along between eras. He arrived in the majors in 1965, just in time to miss the major phase of the Yankees dynasty that went from 1949 to 1964. He joined the Yankees the year after the Bombers lost to the Cardinals in the World Series and played as a semi-regular for two years before joining the starting lineup and establishing himself as a middle-of-the-lineup hitter in 1968.

That year, he hit .267 with 89 runs scored and drew 73 walks, starting a trend that would give him one of the higher on-base percentages in the AL each year. When he retired in 1979, White had a lifetime batting average of .271 and an OBP of .360.

White, who made the All-Star team twice, had his best year in 1970, when the Yankees finished second, after five years in the league's low-rent district. That season he was in the top 15 in AL MVP voting and finished with a .388 OBP and 94 walks, as well as establishing career highs in just about every other category: 296 BA, 22 home runs, 94 RBIs, 288 total bases, 109 runs, 180 hits, and 24 stolen bases.

In 1970, in an article by Mickey Mantle in *Sport Magazine*, Mickey called White one of the most underrated players in baseball. "People ask me, 'What happened to all the Yankees stars?' I tell them that Roy White is as good a player as any of the old players we used to have. He hit for power and average, walked a lot, and he also could steal bases, sacrifice, hit behind the runner, and play the field well."

White was a fixture in the Yankees starting lineup, making over 500 plate appearances every year from 1968 to 1977, and in eight of those years he had more than 600 plate appearances.

In the book *The Bronx Zoo*, pitcher Sparky Lyle said that White was also probably the nicest guy on the team. "He's quiet. He's well respected by everybody and he's very classy."

In his *Historical Baseball Abstract*, historian Bill James rates White as the 25th best left fielder of all time, ranking him ahead of Hall of Famer Jim Rice.

James cites three main reasons for White's being under-appreciated: "1. His skills were subtle and not easily summarized into two or three statistics. 2. Like Ralph Kiner, he was blamed for the failures of his teams. 3. He was measured for much of his career against a standard of Mickey Mantle and Joe DiMaggio."

In a list of the top 50 Yankees of all time, ESPN named Roy White as No. 44.

1. Which Yankees left fielder ran to the wall only to watch Bill Mazeroski's walk-off home run disappear over the fence at Forbes Field in Game 7 of the 1960 World Series?
2. Which Yankees left fielder and World Series hero of the '40s both started and ended his major league career as a pitcher?
   a. Cliff Mapes
   b. Johnny Lindell
   c. Bill Renna
   d. Steve Souchock

3. Who is the Panamanian infielder who was purchased from the A's in 1959, played a lot of left field for the Yankees, and appeared in five consecutive World Series?

4. Which Yankees outfielder was known as "King Kong" (a nickname he hated)?

5. Which Yankees Hall of Fame outfielder was one of the relatively few players in baseball history who batted right-handed and threw left-handed?

6. What was the name of the outfielder from the 1930s and early '40s who played in six World Series for the Yankees and was known as "Twinkletoes"?

7. Which ex-Yankees outfielder managed the Cincinnati Reds to victory in the 1990 World Series?

8. Name the Yankees outfielder who was the MVP of the 2009 World Series.

9. Which Yankees outfielder was born in Curacao and was known as "Bam-Bam"?

10. Which Yankees outfielder led the American League in runs scored in 1985 (146) and 1986 (130)?

Answers
1. Yogi Berra
2. b. Johnny Lindell
3. Hector Lopez
4. Charlie Keller
5. Rickey Henderson
6. George Selkirk
7. Lou Piniella
8. Hideki Matsui
9. Hensley Meulens
10. Rickey Henderson

Six

Center Field

The Rankings!
1. Mickey Mantle
2. Joe DiMaggio
3. Earle Combs
4. Bernie Williams
5. Bobby Murcer
6. Mickey Rivers
7. Johnny Damon
8. Roberto Kelly
9. Whitey Witt
10. Jerry Mumphrey

Now we're talking about the heart of the dynasty.

Joe DiMaggio arrived in 1936 and passed the torch to Mickey Mantle in 1951.

For most of the Yankees Clipper's career he was considered by many to be the best player in baseball. When Mantle played for the Yankees, people said either he or Willie Mays was the best of that post-World War II era. Modern historians are giving the nod to Mays as not only the best player of his time, but of all time. However, that doesn't diminish Mickey's contribution to Yankees teams that won 12 pennants and seven World Series championships. The DiMaggio Yankees went to the World Series 10 times and won nine. And the two were teammates in 1951, a championship year.

DiMaggio finished his career with a .325 average, 361 home runs, 1,537 RBIs (third on the Yankees all time behind Ruth and Gehrig), an OBP of .398, and an OPS of .977.

Compare that to Mantle's .298 average, 536 home runs, 1,509 RBIs (fourth), an OBP of .421, and an OPS identical to DiMaggio's .977.

In Mantle's favor, however, is that Triple Crown in 1956, four home run titles—twice hitting more than 50—the best all-time World Series power numbers, and the fact that he was the most dynamic combination of speed and power in the history of the game, even though his injuries kind of diminished the speed part for a good portion of his career.

DiMaggio has that 56-game hitting streak, the incredible fact that he never struck out as many as 40 times in a season, and the constant reminders about how graceful he was and that he made everything look easy.

They won three MVP awards each, so that's a wash.

Mickey was idolized by his teammates, and it didn't seem like DiMaggio was very close to many of the Yankees, but that was by his choice.

We'll take Mickey by only the narrowest of margins as our No. 1. (Though we understand anyone who gives the nod to DiMaggio.)

Combs is a Hall of Famer, a great hitter who was a table-setter for Gehrig and Ruth from the mid-'20s to the mid-'30s. He led the league in triples three times and scored well-more than 100 runs eight times. But that probably had something to do with Ruth and Gehrig. He retired in 1935.

So, except for the World War II years, the Yankees had a Hall of Famer patrolling center field from 1925 to 1964. Pretty impressive. Then you have Williams and Murcer, who were both underrated and probably had a little below Hall of Fame ability, and Rivers and Damon, who both made major contributions to championship teams.

Bernie Williams

Bernie Williams has to be one of the most unsung heroes in baseball history. He was the cleanup hitter on a team that won four World Series and went to the playoffs almost every year. He won a batting title, played in five All-Star Games, won four Gold Gloves, and set or still holds several career records for postseason play, and yet just four years after his retirement he's still not getting enough respect.

And there's more.

He hit over .300 eight straight years and scored more than 100 runs eight times. He retired with a .297 career batting average, a .381 OBP, 2,336 hits, more than 1,000 walks, 287 home runs, and 1,257 RBIs. He is among the Yankees career leaders in many offensive categories.

Bernie Williams spent seven seasons in the minors before being called up to the Yankees in 1993, but it was worth the wait for both player and team. The speedy outfielder—he had been a world-class 400-meter runner in Puerto Rico as a teen—covered a lot of ground but had a below-average arm and didn't hit for power his first few years in the lineup.

In 1995, he had something of a breakout season with 18 homers, 82 RBIs, and a .307 batting average. He also led the Yankees in runs, hits, total bases, and stolen bases. And he was on fire in the ALDS against the Mariners with a .429 average.

He followed that up with a big 1996, hitting .305, increasing his home run total to 29, and producing the first of five 100-RBI seasons, with 102. His great hitting and fielding earned Williams MVP honors in the ALCS as the Yankees went on to win their first World Series since 1978.

In 1998, Williams reached true stardom on the historic Yankees team that won 114 games, an American League record. That year, he became the first player ever to win a batting title (.339), a Gold Glove Award, and a World Series ring in the same year. After the season the Yankees signed Williams to a 7-year $87.5 million contract, one of the most lucrative in baseball at the time.

The Yankees made the playoffs every year of his contract and Williams finished his career at or near the top of postseason statistics in many categories.

He's played the second-most postseason games ever, with 121 (Jeter is first, with 147, as of 2010), has the most RBIs (80), extra-base hits (51), and he held the record with 22 home runs until it was broken by Manny Ramirez (29).

Toward the end of that long contract his skills began to decline significantly, and the Yankees declined to offer him a new deal. Williams retired following the 2006 season, after 16 years as a Yankee. Today he has a thriving career as a Grammy-award–winning Latin jazz guitarist, so he's doing fine. But it would be nice if he got some of the respect he deserves for a brilliant Yankees career.

Bobby Murcer

Bobby Murcer wanted to only play for the Yankees.

Like Mickey Mantle, he was a highly touted Oklahoman who was signed by Tom Greenwade and was slated to lead the next generation in the late '60s after the retirement of Mantle, his childhood hero.

But the team went into decline after the 1964 World Series loss to the Cardinals, and Murcer, despite having some fine years, didn't get to play in the Series during his prime.

Murcer was a five-time All-Star (four times with the Yankees), who led the American League in on-base percentage in 1971 (.427), the same year he hit a career-high .331. In 1972, he hit 33 home runs, had 96 RBIs, and led the league in runs and total bases.

So his dream of being a star for his favorite team was well on its way.

He was moved to right field when the Yankees gave newcomer Elliot Maddox the center-field job. Though he was reluctant to make the move, Murcer, who thought the center-field job was his, was beginning to adjust to the idea.

A true and loyal Yankee, Murcer never envisioned playing for another team. But, he was traded to the Giants for Bobby Bonds after the 1974 season. "The trade came," Murcer said, "just after I had told Gabe Paul [Yankees general manager] that I could finally accept right field if I knew I would be a Yankee the rest of my career. He said there was no way the Yankees could trade me. Three days later, I was gone." Murcer played in San Francisco for two years, putting up 23 and 27 homers and driving in 90 and 89 runs, respectively, before going to the Cubs in a trade.

He finally returned to the Yankees in 1979 and remained with them until he retired in 1985, having hit 252 home runs and driven in 1,043 runs. In 1981, he was on the Yankees roster for the World Series and pinch-hit three times without a hit.

Murcer remained a Yankee for the rest of his life, as he moved into the broadcast booth, where he became a much-loved and respected member of the Yankees announcing team for many years. He was also known as a generous participant and contributor to numerous charities.

Dave Fultz

Dave Fultz was an outfielder for The Highlanders from 1903–05, the last three years of his seven-year major league career. He's not on our list of top 10 Yankees center fielders, but he was an interesting guy so we thought you'd like to know about him.

Fultz was a fleet fielder (a running back for the football team at Brown) who could steal a base. He stole a career-high 44 bases in 1905, his final year in the big leagues. He was a .271 lifetime hitter in 644 major league games.

In 1902, as a member of the A's, he hit a career-high .302 and led the American League with 109 runs scored. In a game against the Tigers, Fultz stole second, third, and home in the second inning.

Late in September 1905, Fultz broke both his nose and jaw in a collision with teammate Kid Elberfeld and was forced to retire from baseball.

Fultz, who was captain of both his college football and baseball teams, graduated from Brown in 1898 with a law degree. In baseball's off-season he attended New York Law School and passed the New York bar exam. He also served as a college football coach at Missouri, in 1898, and went on to coach at Lafayette, Brown, and NYU while he was still an active major leaguer.

When his baseball playing days were over, he hung out his shingle and became a practicing attorney in New York, and in 1912 he infuriated baseball owners by creating a union of baseball players called the Players Fraternity, with Ty Cobb and Christy Mathewson serving as two of the officers. The Fraternity threatened a strike in 1917, but that was averted when Fultz got some concessions for the players. The union was disbanded during World War I.

During the war Fultz was a lieutenant aviator and later became president of baseball's International League.

He practiced law and had an office in New York until his retirement in 1947.

(Left to right) Roger Maris, Yogi Berra, and Mickey Mantle pose in the dugout before a July 1961 game at Fenway.

Quiz!

1. Joe DiMaggio's brother Dominic was a great center fielder for the Red Sox. What was the name of the third DiMaggio brother who played in the majors?
2. The center fielder on the Yankees' first world championship in 1923 was:
   a. Bob Meusel
   b. Earle Combs
   c. Ben Chapman
   d. Whitey Witt
3. Which outfielder was traded to the Reds for Paul O'Neill in 1993?

4. Which American League outfielder started with the Royals, and starred for the A's, before winning World Series titles with both the Red Sox and the Yankees?

5. Name the two men on this list with more than 1,000 walks as a Yankee.

6. In 1941, the year of Joe DiMaggio's 56-game hitting streak, the Yankee Clipper finished third in the race for the batting title with a .357 average. Ted Williams was first, hitting .406. Who finished in second place?

7. Who won the RBI title that year?

8. How many years did DiMaggio finish in the top 10 in the AL MVP vote?

9. What number did Mickey Mantle wear in his rookie year of 1951, before being sent down to the minors?

10. Mantle won the AL Triple Crown in 1956. Who were the second-place finishers in each of the three categories?

Answers

1. Vince DiMaggio
2. d. Whitey Witt
3. Roberto Kelly
4. Johnny Damon
5. Mickey Mantle and Bernie Williams
6. Cecil Travis of the Senators hit .359.
7. DiMaggio, with 125
8. Ten times, with wins in 1939, '41, and '47.
9. No. 6
10. Batting average: Ted Williams (Red Sox) .345; Home runs: Vic Wertz (Indians) 32; RBIs: Al Kaline (Tigers) 128

Seven

Right Field

The Rankings!
1. Babe Ruth
2. Dave Winfield
3. Reggie Jackson
4. Paul O'Neill
5. Roger Maris
6. Tommy Henrich
7. Willie Keeler
8. Hank Bauer
9. Gary Sheffield
10. Jesse Barfield

To say that the Yankees' right-field job has been in capable hands since the team joined the AL as the Highlanders in 1903 is one of the great understatements in baseball history.

Perhaps no other position on any team has been the home of so many great ballplayers. But more than that, the Yankees dynasty that began with the first pennant in 1921 could not have happened without the contributions made by the men on this list.

There are four members of the Hall of Fame among the Yankees' top 10 right fielders: Ruth, Winfield, Jackson, and Keeler (who played for the Highlanders, who became the Yankees).

Winfield, one of the great all-around players of his time, and our second-place man, never played in a World Series for the Yankees. But Ruth, Jackson, O'Neill, Maris, Henrich, and Bauer played in a combined total of 33 World Series as Yankees, winning 23 championships.

And the Babe isn't even on the top of the list in World Series appearances or World Series won. That honor goes to Bauer, who went to nine World Series and was on the winning side seven times in his Yankees career, between 1948 and 1959.

He was so used to the World Series check every fall that he would come down on any player who was letting his after-hours escapades affect his performance on the field by warning the offender: "Don't mess with my money."

Four of these six right fielders—Ruth, Maris, Jackson, and O'Neill—also won World Series rings as members of other teams.

Ruth, of course, was a great pitcher on three Red Sox title teams in the 1910s, Maris went on to win another world championship with the Cardinals in 1967, Jackson was on the great Oakland A's teams of the early- to mid-'70s and got his World Series rings in 1972 (though he was injured and couldn't play in the Series), '73, and '74. O'Neill was a member of the 1990 Reds team that swept to the title.

Henrich, who played his entire major league career with the Yankees, and Bauer, who was in pinstripes for most of his MLB life, were players who were able to perform at even a higher level in the clutch—and especially in the Fall Classic.

To be fair, Sheffield was on the world champion Marlins team in 1997, before playing for the Yankees, and Winfield finally got his ring in 1992 as a member of the Blue Jays.

But our focus is strictly The Bronx, and so here's a brief look at the six right fielders who helped bring 33 pennants and 23 titles to Yankee Stadium.

Babe Ruth

He started his career as a dominant left-handed pitcher who played on three championship teams in Boston. He won 20 games twice and was 3–0 over two World Series.

But his powerful bat forced the Red Sox to gradually convert him to the outfield so he could be in the lineup every day. As an everyday outfielder in 1919 (he still pitched in 17 games), he hit 29 home runs and drove in 114, which turned out to be only a preview of his awesome offensive presence.

The following year he was sold to the Yankees (generally considered the worst trade of all time), and for the next few seasons the Babe almost single-handedly saved baseball from disaster in the wake of the Black Sox scandal, all while transforming the game by ushering in the "live ball" era.

In his first year with the Yankees, who were the Giants' tenants at the Polo Grounds at the time, he hit 54 homers (a total that was more than every team in baseball but the Phillies) and had a slugging percentage of .847, a record that stood until 2001.

"I hope he lives to hit 100 homers in a season. I wish him all the luck in the world. He has everybody else, including myself, hopelessly outclassed," said his Yankees teammate Frank "Home Run" Baker.

Ruth roared back with 59 home runs in 1921, hitting .378, with a slugging percentage of .846. He had an off-year in 1922, due to injuries, suspensions, and lackluster play.

In both of those seasons, the Yankees made the World Series but lost to McGraw's Giants.

In 1923, Yankee Stadium—The House that Ruth Built—was opened, and Babe christened the beautiful new ballpark by smacking the first home run of the season. The Yankees were the best team in baseball that year, winning the AL pennant by 16 games. With Ruth hitting a career-high .393 and smacking 41 home runs, the Yankees met the Giants in the World Series for the third straight time and the Bambino, who had by now reached full mythical status, really came of age on the big stage.

In the World Series—in which the Yankees won their first world championship four games to two—Ruth had seven hits, three home runs, and scored eight runs. Giants pitchers walked him eight times in the Series.

Thanks to the new stadium, which was the largest in baseball, and the expansion of the Polo Grounds, the Giants' home, the 1923 World Series was the first to top the 300,000 mark in attendance.

The Senators won the AL pennant the next two years. Then, in 1926, with Ruth, an improving Lou Gehrig, and Murderer's Row firmly in place, the Yankees took their first of three pennants in a row. They lost the World Series to the Cardinals that year, before the '27 Yankees—often considered the greatest team of all time—swept the Pirates. They would do the same to the Cardinals the following year.

Of course, 1927 was the year the Babe set the single-season home run record, hitting 60 and combining with Gehrig to lead the team to 110 wins, winning the pennant by a margin of 19 games over the second-place A's.

The A's, led by future Hall of Famers Lefty Grove, Jimmie Foxx, Al Simmons, and Mickey Cochrane, were runners-up in '27 and '28, before winning three pennants in a row. (Though Ruth would lead the league in homers every year.)

A Ruth-led Yankees squad would come back for one more season of glory, winning the pennant in '32 and sweeping the Cubs in a World Series that featured the Bambino's famous called shot.

It was the fifth inning of Game 3 at Wrigley Field. Ruth had been jawing with pitcher Charlie Root and the Cubs' dugout, and with the count 2–2, Ruth pointed, though whether it was at Root or to center field, no one is 100 percent sure. What is known is that Ruth crushed the next pitch—a curveball—440 feet to the deepest part of the center-field bleachers. It would be Ruth's last World Series home run. The controversy over whether Ruth actually called the homer is part of baseball folklore.

Ruth's teammate Bill Dickey once said about Ruth's strength, "He hits a ball harder and farther than any man I ever saw."

Famed pitcher Dizzy Dean thought that the balls the Babe hit had a life of their own. "No one hit home runs the way Babe Ruth did. They were something special. They were like homing pigeons. The ball would leave the bat, pause briefly, suddenly gain its bearings, then take off for the stands."

The Sultan of Swat would play in the first two major league All-Star Games before being sent to Boston of the National League in 1935. He only played part of that season. He did, however, have one more taste of glory, hitting three home runs in a game in Pittsburgh, but he was clearly finished, and he retired five days later.

Babe Ruth is rated by many as the greatest player of all time.

Tommy Henrich

Old Reliable was the Yankees right fielder in the late 1930s and most of the '40s, and he was one of baseball's all-time great clutch hitters. The more important the situation, the more likely it was that Henrich would deliver a big hit or a heads-up play.

In Game 4 of the 1941 World Series, the Yankees were ahead two games to one. They trailed the Dodgers 4–3 in the bottom of the ninth with Henrich at the plate. The count was full and the next pitch by Dodgers pitcher Hugh Casey broke in the dirt as Henrich swung and missed for the third strike. The ball bounced by catcher Mickey

Owen, and the ever-alert Henrich immediately hustled to first base to begin a four-run rally that gave the Yankees a commanding 7–4 lead. They won that game and then Game 5 for the title.

Henrich, a five-time All-Star and four-time World Series champion, continued to be one of the Yankees' most consistent hitters throughout the '40s, minus the three seasons he missed while serving in the Coast Guard during World War II.

But there were still more World Series heroics for Old Reliable, who became known for getting crucial hits. In the 1947 Series, again against the Dodgers, Henrich helped win Game 1 with a pair of RBIs and Game 2 with a solo homer. In Game 7, he broke a 2–2 tie by driving in Phil Rizzuto with the game-winning RBI.

In 1949, Henrich posted a pair of RBIs in a 5–3 win over the Red Sox on the last day of the season to win the pennant by one game. And in the Series that year he won Game 1 with a homer off Don Newcombe to lead off the ninth inning, the first walk-off home run in Series history. He also scored twice in the fifth game, a 10–6 Yankees win that ended the series.

During his career, Henrich, along with Joe DiMaggio and Charlie Keller, formed one of the greatest outfields of all time. And nobody in Yankees history expressed a more passionate love for baseball or more loyalty to the Yankees pinstripes.

Henrich, who was also a fine fielder, expressed his serious take on the game when he said, "Catching a fly ball is a pleasure, but knowing what to do with it after you catch it is a business."

"Tommy was an extremely smart player," said teammate Bobby Brown. "He was always thinking about how to do the right thing at the right time. He knew the nuances of every outfield wall in the league and worked on figuring out caroms and positioning himself to get a quick release."

Henrich was a .282 lifetime hitter who twice led the league in triples and once in runs. He knocked in 80 runs or more six times, with a high of 100 in 1948. And he hit more than 20 homers four times, with a high of 31 in 1941.

Bob Feller once paid tribute to Henrich when he said, "That guy can hit me in the middle of the night, blindfolded and with two broken feet, to boot."

Hank Bauer

This three-time All-Star was a leader on the great Yankees teams from 1949 to 1959. He played in nine World Series and was on the winning side seven times. He could do everything well. His toughness and leadership were key elements on those great teams.

"Hank could hit and he was a great fielder with a terrific arm," said former Yankee Bill Skowron. "And he didn't take any crap from anyone. He was a vocal leader in the clubhouse. He had been a marine. He always played hard."

"Bauer was another one of those players who was at his best in big games," said Bobby Brown. "He was a player who could do everything. He had good speed, a great arm, he was smart, and he stayed healthy. He murdered left-handed pitching."

Bauer was a genuine war hero. He was a lieutenant in the marines who served in the Pacific, during which time he went through a bout of malaria, earned 11 campaign ribbons, two Bronze Stars, and two Purple Hearts.

"He was a tough dude," said pitcher Don Larsen about Bauer. "He helped a lot of people get used to that New York environment. He was a tough person. Thank God he wasn't mean. When he walked onto that field, business started."

"When he was on the field, you were his enemy," said Yogi Berra. "Off the field he was...one of the nicest guys you'd ever want to meet. But on the field, it was his job."

In describing Bauer's ruggedness and tough demeanor, someone once said his face looked like a closed fist.

"When Hank came down that base path, the whole earth trembled," said Red Sox infielder Johnny Pesky.

Bauer had a .277 lifetime batting average, 164 home runs, and 703 RBIs. Not only that, but he performed in the postseason. In World Series play he had 46 hits, seven home runs, and 25 RBIs, and he still holds the record for the longest hitting streak in the World Series, with 17 games.

In the sixth and final game of the 1951 World Series, Bauer hit a three-run triple, and he saved the game with a diving catch for the final out.

Roger Maris

If the other players on this list of World Series right fielders were known for their passion, their colorful personalities, and their leadership abilities, then Roger Maris stands out. He was just a small-town family man who was doing his job, extremely well.

It's become a buzz phrase in recent years to talk about someone who delivers more quality than promised as "exceeding our expectations." They weren't using that phrase in 1960, but it certainly applied to the Yankees new outfielder Roger Maris, who exceeded expectations perhaps more than any player in history.

In his three years in the majors before joining the Yankees, Maris never hit more than 28 home runs or drove in more than 80 runs.

At 25, he was a promising young hitter who seemed to be a suitable replacement for Bauer, who went to Kansas City in the off-season trade that brought Maris to New York before the 1960 season.

But, who could ever have known how talented Maris really was?

In his first two years with the Yankees, he hit 39 and then 61 home runs to break Babe Ruth's single-season home run record that had stood for 34 years. He also knocked in 112 and then 141 runs. And for his efforts, Maris was named the league's MVP both years.

Maris' talents didn't end with his batting, as he was also a fine right fielder who often made catches that observers gave up on as sure homers or extra-bases hits. When needed, Maris filled in for Mickey Mantle in center field, He had the range and the arm to handle any outfield position.

Who would have expected Maris to be that good?

Casey Stengel once appraised Maris' abilities as only Casey could: "I give the man a point for speed. I do this because Maris can run fast. Then I can give him a point because he can slide fast. I give him another point because he can bunt. I also give him a point because he can field. He is very good around the fences—sometimes on top of the fences. Next I give him a point because he can throw. A right fielder has to be able to throw or he's not a right fielder. So, I add up my points and I've got five for him before I even come to his hitting. I would say this is a good man."

So at least Casey seemed to know what the Yankees had in Maris.

Though Maris was the focus of national attention in 1961, when he was in pursuit of Ruth's record of 60 home runs, he was not popular with the press and the fans for several reasons.

Many of the older New York writers remembered the Bambino and wanted to see his record stand. At least they didn't want it broken by a man they considered a run-of-the-mill ballplayer like Maris.

Better that Yankees hero Mickey Mantle, whom the press wasn't really crazy about before Maris came along, be the man to break the record. So in the "M&M" home run chase, many writers and fans were rooting for Mickey.

But, Maris is certainly responsible for some of the negative press.

He was a private man, a small-town guy who didn't particularly like the bright lights and tempo of the big city. He was not the kind of man who sought the spotlight. The more attention he got the less cooperative he became, and his relationship with many members of the press deteriorated into one of mutual hostility. While he was handling the pressure as a ballplayer, he was knuckling under to the more intense pressure of being a public figure.

Maris didn't receive much support from the Yankees that year, either.

There were no press conferences or publicity department statements, nothing to shield him from the constant barrage of repetitious questions that made him surly and uncooperative. Maris' reputation never recovered from that experience.

But Maris did win a pair of MVPs while contributing to seven runs to the World Series, counting his two years as the Cardinals' right fielder later in the decade. And he did hold the record for most home runs in a season for 37 seasons. (Ruth held it for 34.) Plus, when other players did hit more than 61 homers, they were players who apparently took some "extraordinary measures" to accomplish the feat. In fact, many purists still consider Maris' 61 as the unofficial record.

Reggie Jackson

Looking back on Reggie Jackson's career it seems as though he was a Yankee for over a decade, but in fact, all the noise, all the heroics, all the words written about the Bronx Zoo took place in five years.

The slugger, who came out of the Philadelphia area as a multi-sport star, signed with the Yankees before the 1977 season, already established as one of the great power hitters for a decade, mostly with the A's, who won three World Series in that time. Jackson had been the AL MVP in 1971, when he hit 32 round-trippers and drove in 117 runs, and he was selected as the MVP of the World Series triumph over the Mets in 1973.

So, when he came to the Big Apple, Jackson was not in awe of New York or the Yankees tradition.

"I didn't come to New York to be a star, I brought my star with me," declared Jackson.

The Yankees had won the pennant the year before, but lost to the Big Red Machine in the World Series, and Reggie was viewed by George Steinbrenner as the piece of the puzzle that would put them over the top.

But when Reggie was quoted as saying to a reporter that "I'm the straw that stirs the drink," it was interpreted as a knock on captain and established team leader Thurman Munson, and it put the 31-year-old Jackson in some conflict with Munson and his devoted teammates.

That first season was marked by some serious conflicts with volatile manager Billy Martin, including an embarrassing confrontation in the dugout that was caught by the TV cameras after the skipper removed Reggie from a game for allegedly failing to hustle in the field.

Reggie blasted 32 homers in that season of the Bronx Zoo, and he drove in 110 runs, but he was unbelievable in the World Series. Against the Dodgers in that autumn of '77, Jackson had nine hits in 20 at-bats, for an average of .450. He also hit five home runs to go along with eight RBIs, including three dingers on the first pitch off three different pitchers in Game 6. That made Jackson the only man other than Babe Ruth to hit three home runs in a single World Series game. Reggie became the first player to be named MVP of the Series for two different teams, and that Fall Classic performance solidified his nickname of "Mr. October."

The 1978 season saw one of the great Yankees comebacks of all time, after they were behind the Red Sox by 13 games in July.

Reggie had 27 home runs and 97 RBIs that season, and once again he came up big in the World Series with a pair of home runs and eight RBIs.

In his career, Jackson hit 10 homers and knocked in 24 runs in the World Series, with a batting average of .357 and an OBP of .457. His final tally for the postseason was 18 home runs and 48 RBIs.

"October, that's when they pay off for playing ball," Jackson once said.

Jackson was elected to baseball's Hall of Fame in 1993.

Paul O'Neill

How could anyone know when they traded for him in 1992 that Paul O'Neill would become a Yankees great, who may someday get his No. 21 retired by the team?

O'Neill was considered a pretty good player during his eight-year stint with the Reds. He was a member of their 1990 world championship team and he did have one outstanding season, 1991, when he hit 28 home runs and knocked in 91. But nobody predicted how deeply he would carve his name in Yankees history.

The right fielder from Ohio made himself at home in Yankee Stadium, won a batting title, and became a leader on a team that dominated baseball in the late '90s, winning four titles and making the playoffs seven straight years.

Paul O'Neill was the emotional heart of the Yankees through the '90s' dynasty.

When he arrived in 1993 the Yankees hadn't been to the playoffs since 1981, but with O'Neill in the outfield they had a seven-year run in the postseason that included four World Series. O'Neill wasn't one of those efficient, businesslike players who were responsible for quips such as, "rooting for the Yankees is like rooting for General Motors." The Warrior—as he was known—wore his emotions on his sleeve. He was visibly upset when he struck out to end a rally or committed a faux pas in the field. He destroyed water coolers and threw bats on the field, and the fans loved him for that just as much as for the outstanding record he built in those nine years.

The Yankees acquired O'Neill when he was 30 years old and he contributed immediately, hitting .311 in his first season, with 20 home runs and 75 RBIs in 1993. In his second year, the strike-shortened season of 1994, he was the American League batting champion, hitting .359 with 21 homers and 83 RBIs.

His consistency was uncanny, as he hit between 18 and 24 homers every year, averaged 100 RBIs a year, and carried a .303 batting average.

He helped the Yankees to their world championships in 1996, '98, '99, and 2000, and he was loved by the fans for his fiery personality and his competitiveness.

He was never satisfied with his own performance.

O'Neill said it was easier for him to play in New York than in Cincinnati, because he grew up in Columbus and his whole family was there. His first five years he played for his boyhood idol, Pete Rose. "It's tough to play in your hometown," he told author Jack O'Connell. "Everybody in town knows all about you and looks over your shoulder every day. In New York, I could just come to the Stadium, play, and go home. Playing in New York really worked out for me, it was the best time of my life."

O'Neill is the only player in history to have played on the winning side of three perfect games, with two of them coming at Yankee Stadium. He was in the field for David Wells' perfect game on May 17, 1998, and for David Cone's on July 18, 1999. The other was by the Reds' Tom Browning on September 16, 1988, at Cincinnati's Riverfront Stadium.

In the last inning of Game 5 of the 2001 World Series, O'Neill, who had already announced his retirement, was in right field when the entire stadium crowd, in a display of affection, began chanting his name and kept it up even as he ran to the dugout at the end of the inning.

A teary O'Neill tipped his cap to the crowd, which prompted a roar of appreciation.

"The sense of history at Yankee Stadium, you don't get in other parks," O'Neill said. "I played at Fenway Park and Wrigley Field, but they're not Yankee Stadium. I got to meet Mickey Mantle and shake hands with Joe DiMaggio. I played with Don Mattingly and Mariano Rivera and Derek Jeter. I went to the postseason seven years in a row, and I always felt the fans here were behind me all the way."

That O'Neill and Yankees fans would develop such a relationship seemed remote when he arrived from Cincinnati in 1993 after being traded in the previous off-season. New Yorkers knew him from his Reds days as a moody .259 hitter who just might melt under the pressure that comes with playing in the Big Apple. O'Neill had an early ally in the city in his sister, Molly, the food critic for the *New York Times*, but he gradually won over Yankees fans with his intensity. He was sort of an Irish version of Lou Piniella, his former Reds manager, another temperamental outfielder who was adored by Yankees crowds.

Quiz!

1. Which Yankees right fielder had a candy bar named for him?
   a. Dave Winfield
   b. Al Snickers
   c. Reggie Jackson
   d. Roger Maris
2. The Yankees got Roger Maris in a trade with which American League team?

3. Which of the 10 right fielders on this list went on to manage an American League team to a World Series title?
4. One man on this list is a native New Yorker. Who is it?
5. In 1927, the year that Babe Ruth hit 60 home runs, he didn't win the RBI title. Who did?
6. In 1961, the year Roger Maris broke Babe Ruth's record with 61 homers, five of his Yankees teammates hit more than 20 home runs. Name these five Yankees. (Bonus: how many did each hit?)
7. Who is the Red Sox right-hander who served up Roger Maris' 61ˢᵗ home run in 1961?
8. Name the outfielder the Yankees sent to the Reds in exchange for Paul O'Neill.
9. What character on which sitcom asked O'Neill to hit two home runs in a game for a little boy who was in the hospital? (Bonus: what's the name of the episode?)
10. Which left-handed pitcher served up Babe Ruth's 60ᵗʰ home run in 1927?

Eight

Catcher

The Rankings!
1. Yogi Berra
2. Bill Dickey
3. Thurman Munson
4. Elston Howard
5. Jorge Posada
6. Wally Schang
7. Rick Cerone
8. Butch Wynegar
9. Mike Stanley
10. Joe Girardi

Contrary to popular belief, Bill Dickey was not a member of the 1927 Murderers Row Yankees. He made his first major league appearance in 1928 and got the starting job in 1929. He held that job through the 1930s and early '40s, starting on seven world champion teams and setting a standard for excellence for Yankees catchers that continues to this day.

Dickey was the first, and when he retired he mentored an awkward Yogi Berra, helping to turn Yogi into a great defensive catcher. Elston Howard, Thurman Munson, and most recently, Jorge Posada, carry on the Yankees tradition of greatness with the "tools of ignorance."

Others, especially Wally Schang, who preceded Dickey, held the job with some distinction for shorter periods of time, but these five all played at a Hall of Fame level, even though the latter three may be judged to lack the career numbers to be elected to Cooperstown.

Many Yankees supporters believe the selection of Howard and Munson and eventually Posada in the Hall of Fame would be a fitting tribute to their achievements on multiple championship teams.

Thurman Munson

After winning the American League pennant from 1960-64, the Yankees were way down in the standings for the five years starting in 1965. They finished sixth, tenth, ninth, fifth, and fifth. Then, in 1970, the year the brash young Ohioan Thurman Munson made the starting catcher's job his own, there was a jump to second place.

While we're not saying he was totally responsible for the improvement, it is evident that the Yankees were in much better shape with a catcher who carried the legacy of Yankees greats such as Bill Dickey, Yogi Berra, and Elston Howard.

After a slow start in his rookie year, Munson finished with a .302 batting average and won the AL Rookie of the Year Award. The following year Munson made the first of his seven All-Star teams. That year, the Red Sox's Carlton Fisk won rookie honors, thus beginning a fierce rivalry between two great catchers with powerful personalities.

Munson proved himself to be a fine hitter as well as an agile catcher.

In a career that lasted 11 years and ended tragically in a private plane accident in 1979, he was the AL most valuable player in 1976 and finished with a .292 career batting average (hitting over .300 five times).

Defensively, he was quick and agile behind the plate, winning three Gold Gloves. He probably had the quickest release of any catcher in baseball.

"He had so much energy behind the plate," said Buck Martinez, a former catcher and later a broadcaster. "He was kind of awkward and crude in what he did, but he was good. And he had the personality to lead his pitching staff."

"He didn't have a great arm," said Don Zimmer, "but...he could throw guys out because he was quick as a cat. He was an outstanding catcher because he knew the game. He was a great hitter."

Mel Stottlemyre, who pitched to Munson in the early 1970s, was quoted by The Baseball Page.com: "He was so sure of himself, and so sure of what he could do behind the plate. He was as quick as anybody I've ever seen coming out from behind that crouch on bunted balls and on his throws to second."

A common description of Munson was that he was "tough as nails" or that he was "a real blood and guts kind of guy." Everybody you speak to about him mentions his leadership and his clutch hitting. He played through numerous injuries to his legs, arms, and shoulders.

His fiery temperament established him quickly as the team leader and the face of a new competitive Yankees ballclub that won three pennants and a pair of World Series later in the decade. His leadership and his influence on the team were discussed by former teammate Elliot Maddox in a quote on The Baseball Page.com: "If Thurman was on your case and telling you, 'You have to apply yourself more, you have to do this,' or 'You have to do that because you know you're capable of it,' it meant he liked you. So, he loved me because he never gave me a moment's peace. So, you would want to do it just to get him off your back."

Munson was a clutch hitter, too. In 14 ALCS games, Munson hit two home runs, knocked in 10 runs, and batted .339. And in the World Series he was even better, batting .373, with one home run and 12 RBIs. In the 1976 World Series, Munson hit .529 with six hits in his last six at-bats.

After the Yankees were swept in the 1976 World Series, owner George Steinbrenner went out and signed Reggie Jackson, who was supposed to be the last piece of the puzzle. Steinbrenner turned out to be correct about Jackson, but Reggie's arrival started immediate controversy with Munson, who was the team's first captain since Lou Gehrig.

First of all, Jackson was paid more than Munson, and Steinbrenner had assured Munson that he would always be the highest-paid Yankee. Then Reggie launched the bombshell that touched off a tense period for the team.

He was quoted in *Sport Magazine* as saying, "I'm the straw that stirs the drink. It all comes back to me. Maybe I should say me and Munson. But he doesn't enter into it. He can only stir it bad."

Even though Jackson claimed he was misquoted, Munson was furious with Reggie and with the press, but the team won the next two World Series and the two players eventually made up and became quite friendly.

In his final two years, the injuries and the wear and tear on his body from catching every day began to take their toll. Munson's production began to decline, and he even spoke about retirement.

After he died, there was some talk by the baseball writers in New York of getting the five-year Hall of Fame waiting period waived so Munson could be admitted sooner, but it never went through, and Munson's support for the hall has declined over the years.

Fisk is a Hall of Famer, due to his longevity, his power numbers, and because he was acknowledged as the best defensive catcher of his time.

"Fisk and Munson were the two premier catchers of their era in the American League," said Jim Kaat, who was a member of the Yankees when Munson was killed. "It's just unfortunate Munson didn't get to play longer."

This is what former major leaguer, Yankee announcer, and National League president Bill White had to say in his recent book *Uppity, My Life in Baseball*, about Yankee catcher Thurman Munson

"I saw a lot of talented players during my years as a Yankee broadcaster: Catfish Hunter, Reggie Jackson, Goose Gossage, Rickey Henderson, and many others. But the consistently best Yankee player I ever knew was catcher Thurman Munson…. Munson was without question the most intelligent catcher in the American League, with a great sense of command in calling pitchers and an ability to both challenge and calm pitchers he worked with. He had those unique qualities that make a man a leader."

Wally Schang

This catcher, who could hit, run, throw, and play excellent defense, spent 19 years in the majors and was a member of seven pennant-winning teams. He was an important member of World Series champions with the A's, Red Sox, and Yankees.

Schang had a .284 lifetime batting average and a .393 OBP, and he threw out nine runners in the 1921 World Series.

Historian Bill James rates Schang as the 20th best catcher of all time in *The New Bill James Baseball Historical Abstract*.

Schang, who over the years has received strong consideration as a Hall of Fame candidate by the veterans committee, was at the center of American League history during his career, having served as a battery mate for Hall of Fame pitchers Eddie Plank, Chief Bender, Babe Ruth, Herb Pennock, Waite Hoyt, and Lefty Grove. Wally was particularly adept at handling pitching staffs and he had a rifle for an arm.

Before the 1913 World Series between the Giants and the A's, sportswriter Hugh Fullerton wrote a column comparing Schang to Giants catcher Chief Meyers. "Defensively, Schang has proved one of the wonders of the year," Fullerton writes. "Wally has cut down 50 percent of the runners attempting to steal." Schang was the sensation of the 1913 World Series, as he hit .357 and had seven RBIs.

Then, in the pennant-winning year of 1914, the A's catcher got a great deal of support for the Chalmers Award, the MVP of its day.

On May 15, 1915, Schang nailed six Browns runners who tried to steal. Then, exactly five years later as a member of the Red Sox, he had eight assists against the Indians. Both are major league records.

When Schang joined the Red Sox in 1917, Ruth was still a member of the pitching staff. Management soon decided that Ruth's bat was needed in the lineup, so he played a lot of outfield between starts.

Schang was great yet again in the Red Sox World Series victory over the Cubs. Over the next few years the Red Sox sent many prominent players to the Yankees. The most famous was Ruth, but Schang was no throw-in.

He was the Yankees starting catcher in their first three pennants and was there for the opening year of Yankee Stadium, serving as the catcher on the Yankees' first championship team in 1923.

He's the only catcher to have started for three different championship teams

Yogi Berra

Yogi Berra's World Series record is something all children should learn when they become interested in baseball. It is truly extraordinary.

- Yogi played in more World Series than any player in baseball history (14), and he has been on the winning side (the Yankees) 10 times, which is more than anyone.
- He played in more World Series games (75) than any player in baseball history.
- He holds the record for most hits in the World Series, with 71.
- He has the most at-bats, with 259.
- He has the most games caught, with 63.
- He hit 12 World Series home runs and drove in 39 World Series runs. That total includes 10 RBIs in 1956 and 8 in 1960.
- He's tied with Frankie Frisch for most World Series career doubles, with 10.
- He's second to Mickey Mantle in World Series runs scored, 42 to 41.
- He has also hit both a World Series grand slam and pinch-hit home run.
- Oh, and he played in the All-Star Game for 15 consecutive years.

Art Jorgens

You've probably never heard of Arndt "Art" Jorgens. Few of today's baseball fans have. In fact, Jorgens was probably not known to many fans during his own time. But Jorgens, a reserve catcher for the New York Yankees, shares a distinction with his more illustrious teammates such as Lou Gehrig, Joe DiMaggio, and Bill Dickey. They all played their entire careers for the Bronx Bombers, which is a claim not even the great Babe Ruth could make.

Jorgens was in a Yankees uniform from 1929 to 1939 as the backup catcher to Hall of Fame member Dickey. It was one of the great Yankees eras that saw them win the World Series six times.

Though he was active for five Fall Classics, he never made an appearance in any of them. And he holds the record for most games on a World Series roster (23) without ever getting into a game. He didn't make the postseason roster in 1933.

The most he ever caught during a season was 56 games, which he did in both 1932 and 1934, when Dickey was injured. Jorgens came to the plate just 738 times in 11 years, an average of 67 at-bats per season, and he retired with four home runs and 89 RBIs to his credit.

While at bat he was someone who could wait out a walk. His .238 lifetime batting average swells to a .317 OBP. We have to assume that he was a pretty good defensive catcher, and that he could call a good game, for a great team like the Yankees to have entrusted him with the backup role for 11 years.

So, in tribute to his patience and his ability to answer the call when he was needed, we salute Art Jorgens and give him one more taste of glory.

Quiz!

1. Which catcher backed up Yogi Berra for several years and later became a Yankees manager, piloting the team to two World Series titles?
2. Which Yankees catcher of the 1960s and early '70s was an All-American quarterback at Mississippi, and was elected to the College Football Hall of Fame?
3. Which catcher came up with the Yankees as Thurman Munson's backup in 1972 before going on to have two productive years as the Indians' starter?
4. Which catcher started on world championship teams with the A's and the Red Sox before taking over the Yankees job in 1921?

5. Which Yankees catcher played in five World Series and was behind the plate when Bill Mazeroski hit the home run to give the Pirates the 1960 World Series?

6. Butch Wynegar came in second in the AL Rookie of the Year voting in 1976. Who won that year?

7. Three Yankees catchers have won a total of five AL MVP awards. Who are they, and in what years did they win the awards?

8. Who were the three catchers on the 1927 Yankees?

9. Who was the only other catcher besides Jorge Posada who played for the Yankees in the 2009 World Series?

10. In 1938, Bill Dickey was second in the AL MVP voting. Who was the winner that year?

Answers
1. Ralph Houk
2. Jake Gibbs
3. Charlie Spikes
4. Wally Schang
5. Johnny Blanchard
6. Mark "the Bird" Fidrych
7. Yogi Berra (1951, '54, and '55); Elston Howard (1963); and Thurman Munson (1976)
8. Pat Collins, Johnny Grabowski, and Benny Bengough
9. Jose Molina
10. Jimmie Foxx, of the Red Sox

Nine

Pitcher

The Rankings!

Starters
1. Whitey Ford
2. Andy Pettitte
3. Ron Guidry
4. Red Ruffing
5. Lefty Gomez
6. Mel Stottlemyre
7. Herb Pennock
8. Allie Reynolds
9. Vic Raschi
10. Waite Hoyt
11. Mike Mussina
12. Jack Chesbro
13. Ed Lopat
14. Roger Clemens
15. Carl Mays
16. Catfish Hunter
17. CC Sabathia
18. Russ Ford
19. Bob Shawkey
20. Fritz Peterson
21. David Cone
22. Ralph Terry
23. Bob Turley
24. Spud Chandler
25. "Sad" Sam Jones
26. Urban Shocker
27. Ed Figueroa
28. George Pipgras
29. Jimmy Key
30. Tommy Byrne

Relievers
1. Mariano Rivera
2. Goose Gossage
3. Joe Page
4. Dave Righetti
5. Sparky Lyle
6. Johnny Murphy
7. Johnny Sain
8. Luis Arroyo
9. John Wetteland
10. Lindy McDaniel

Of course, the Yankees always had good pitching. And management always had the knack for extracting the best years out of pitchers and discarding them before they went downhill. There are only a few career Yankees pitchers who stuck around for the duration and had long careers with the team. Those people at the top of the list—Ford, Pettitte, Guidry, Ruffing, Gomez, and Stottlemyre—were among the notable long-term Yankees. Even the three aces of the 1949 to 1953 teams—Reynolds, Raschi, and Lopat—spent a relatively short time with the club outside of those championship years.

The starting lineup was always filled with superstars, and while the pitching had its share of greats throughout the past, the team's genius has been in getting the pitchers needed to complement that awesome lineup. Such greats as Carl Mays, Urban Shocker, Catfish Hunter, David Cone, Randy Johnson, and Roger Clemens came in, did their job to contribute to Yankees history for a few years, and then moved on.

The Yankees have had their share of top-flight relievers through the pennant runs, but the clear No. 1 is that "freak of nature" Mariano Rivera, who's been dominating the game for the past 16 years. No closer in baseball history has lasted as long and continued to dominate that consistently. It is generally agreed that he's the greatest closer of all time.

Johnny Sain

It's time to revive talk of putting Johnny Sain in the Hall of Fame.

Sain, who gets a lot of credit for being the greatest pitching coach of all time, should take his rightful place in Cooperstown for helping many pitchers achieve their best years while he was their mentor. Sain was a near Hall of Famer as a right-handed pitcher, having won 20 games four times and helping to lead the Boston Braves to the World Series in 1948.

He was half the subject of the famous baseball poem—*Spahn and Sain/and pray for rain*—that described the Braves pitching staff in the drive to the pennant in 1948.

He was the ace of the staff that year, with a 24–14 record, a 2.60 ERA, and a league-leading 28 complete games and 314.2 innings pitched. He finished second to Stan Musial in the MVP voting.

Sain is also famous for squaring off with the Indians' Bob Feller in a classic battle of aces in Game 1 of the '48 World Series. Sain pitched a 4-hitter and won 1–0. In losing, Feller allowed only two hits.

As a footnote to history, Sain was also the last batter to pitch to Babe Ruth—which he did during a charity exhibition game in 1943—and he was the first to pitch to Jackie Robinson in the major leagues when Robinson stepped up for his first major league at-bat on that historic day in 1947.

Southpaw Spahn, who won 20 games or more 13 times in his career, was 15–12 with a 3.71 ERA and 16 complete games in 1948.

They were both good-hitting pitchers who could pinch-hit on days they weren't on the mound. Though Sain had a lifetime batting average of .242 to Spahn's .194, the lefty did hit 35 home runs in his career.

Sain was traded to the Yankees in 1951 and helped them to three World Series titles, operating as both a starter and a reliever. He led the league in saves in 1954, with 22. He retired in 1955 with a resume that also included three All-Star Game selections.

But the subject of this section is John Sain the pitching coach. He held that position with the Royals, Yankees, Twins, Tigers, White Sox, and Braves, along the way helping many pitchers to 20-win seasons. Among his protégés were Whitey Ford, Ralph Terry, Jim Bouton, Mudcat Grant, Jim Kaat, Earl Wilson, Denny McLain, Mickey Lolich, Stan Bahnsen, and Wilbur Wood.

Sain coached pitching staffs on championship teams in New York and Detroit, as well as a pennant winner in Minnesota. He was appointed by Ralph Houk as the Yankees' pitching coach in 1961, and his success was immediate. His first move was to convince Houk to go with a four-man rotation because Sain believed that "pitchers should pitch."

In Sain's three years in pinstripes, the Yankees won three pennants and two World Series. Whitey Ford, who credits Sain with turning him from a good pitcher to a great pitcher, had his first 20-win season in 1961, posting a 25–4 record and 3.21 ERA, not to mention earning his only Cy Young Award.

Ralph Terry had his only 20-win season while working with Sain (23 victories in 1962), and young Jim Bouton, who calls Sain the greatest pitching coach who ever lived and who strongly believes that Sain belongs in the Hall of Fame, had a career year with a 21–7 record and a 2.53 ERA in 1963.

"John was much more than a pitching coach," Bouton said recently. "He was a philosopher. His genius was in how he treated players. He spent time working with rookies, with guys who were struggling. He wasn't a front-runner like a lot of coaches in those days."

Bouton remembers that Sain had a calm perspective.

"He believed that you don't get too high when you win and not too low when you lose," said Bouton. "He'd say the world doesn't want to hear about the labor pains, it just wants to see the baby."

According to Bouton, Sain always stood up for his pitchers, and the pitchers loved him for that.

"He'd always find something positive to say," said Bouton. "If you were knocked out of a game he would come up to you and tell you, 'You really threw a heck of a curve to that No. 4 hitter.' He'd always give you something good to think about."

Sain had frequent run-ins with team managers over such subjects as how much pitchers had to run in the outfield every day.

"John believed you got your legs conditioned more by throwing than by running," said Jim Kaat, who put Sain's teachings into practice when he served as the Reds' pitching coach for a year. "He believed that you had your best chance to win if you got your best pitcher to the mound 42 times a season instead of 32."

Kaat remembers Sain helping Jim Perry when the Twins had given up on him.

"They worked on some mechanical things but really worked to build Jim's confidence," said Kaat. "He would assure Perry that he could get out any hitter in the league. He made Jim believe in himself, and Perry went out and went 8-0 when he was needed to step up because Camilo Pascual was hurt."

Sain was way ahead of his time in instructional methods, using videotape and working as a kind of sports psychologist, according to Kaat. "He put you in a good mental state. If I had John as my pitching coach, I would have been in the Hall of Fame a long time ago. John definitely belongs in Cooperstown."

"John always had some little bit of advice that would help you," Bouton said. "He even advised me to wear my sanitary socks inside-out so the seam wouldn't rub against my skin and cause a blister. That's just an example about how detailed he was and how smart he was about every aspect of baseball. He was just a wonderful man."

Jim Kaat

Jim Kaat, who now works as a broadcaster for the Major League Baseball Network, was a great left-handed pitcher in the major leagues for 25 seasons. He won 20 games three times and finished with a 283–237 record.

Long regarded as one of the best-fielding pitchers of all time, Kaat won an incredible 16 Gold Gloves. He pitched for the Yankees for parts of two seasons and served for a time as a Yankees broadcaster.

We asked Kitty for his comments about many of the left-handers on our Yankees all-time pitching list.

Ed Lopat: He was one of my favorite pitching coaches. At Minnesota he taught me how to throw and use my curveball. He was a great communicator. Eddie wouldn't even get a tryout today because he couldn't throw hard enough to blacken your rear. He threw a variety of off-speed pitches. When old baseball guys talk about a "junk-baller," one of the first names they come up with is Ed Lopat.

Whitey Ford: He was the consummate pitcher. He had command of all his pitches—sinkers, curves, a slider, and he had a good pickoff move. He was particularly great in the big games and in the World Series.

Tommy John: His career parallels mine. Tommy wasn't an exceptionally hard thrower, but he had that great curveball. And, of course, he's famous for coming back from the surgery on his elbow that was named after him.

Ron Guidry: Gator was the Steve Carlton for the Yankees, [but] with a little more power. He had a devastating slider that Sparky Lyle taught him. He got right-handed hitters out on pitches that seemed to be strikes but turned out to be late-breaking balls in the dirt. And he had an excellent fastball to complement his slider. Power guys like Gator have historically had periods of brilliance, but it's difficult to maintain that power over an extended period of time. Guys like Ford who relied on technique and a variety of pitches usually had longer careers.

Ron Guidry delivers a pitch during Game 4 of the 1977 World Series against the Dodgers.

Dave Righetti: Rags was a teammate of mine. He was a hard thrower with strikeout stuff. He was a versatile pitcher who was a great starter and went on to become a great closer. He was a left-handed version of what John Smoltz later became.

David Wells: Boomer was blessed with a rubber arm and a very, very fluid motion that helped him throw strikes better than just about anybody. He had good command of his fastball and threw a high percentage of strikes. He was always a leader in fewest walks per nine innings. He was never stressful on his arm. He was very durable.

Jimmy Key: He reminded me of Whitey. He was considered "crafty," which meant he wasn't a hard thrower. He could really make his curve move. He had some awfully effective years."

Andy Pettitte: Both physically and the way he threw early in his career, Andy reminds me of the way I used to pitch. We were comparable. But he came up with a cutter and that made him successful to the point that he should get consideration for the Hall of Fame. Andy thrived on the urgency of winning in New

York, particularly in the postseason. Like Whitey Ford, he wasn't intimidated by it.

Randy Johnson: He did it with raw power. To his credit, he learned how to control his pitches, and with a big body that's not easy to do. Once he developed a repeatable motion he was next to unhittable. I know that at 6'5" I had a few mechanical issues in trying to keep my arm in sync with my body. Randy learned to do that very well.

CC Sabathia: Of all these pitchers, CC may have the best changeup. That surprises people who look at how big he is and figure he's going to be just a hard thrower. He's a pitcher, he's got a good fastball and a good breaking ball, but that changeup is his big weapon. The key to his longevity will be if he can get his weight under control the next few years. You have to get a little leaner to maintain your flexibility. By the time I was 36, I had gotten down to 210 from 240.

Jim Kaat: I like to think I was dependable. I filled a variety of roles. Stuff-wise, I didn't throw exceptionally hard. I had a fastball and good control. I wasn't dominant except for a year or two, but I was pretty consistent over a number of years. The team could depend on me for 35–40 starts and 250–300 innings. And then I adapted to relief.

A final note. Only three Yankees pitchers have thrown perfect games, and only two of those took place in the regular season.

- Don Larsen, October 8, 1956: 2–0 over the Dodgers in Game 5 of the 1956 World Series at Yankee Stadium (only perfect game in World Series history).
- David Wells, May 17, 1998: 4–0 over the Twins at Yankee Stadium.
- David Cone, July 18, 1999: 6–0 over the Montreal Expos at Yankee Stadium.

Quiz!

1. Which Yankees right-hander was the 1954 AL Rookie of the Year?
   a. Johnny Kucks
   b. Bob Grim
   c. Ralph Terry
   d. Bob Turley

2. Which one of the following players was a southpaw?
   a. Tommy Byrne
   b. Tom Sturdivant
   c. Tom Gorman
   d. Tom Morgan

3. Which ex-Yankee left-hander was on the mound when Hank Aaron hit his 715th career home run to break Babe Ruth's record?

4. Which 30-year-old rookie won 19 games for the '27 Yankees, while tying for the league lead in saves, with 13?
   a. Wilcy Moore
   b. Myles Thomas
   c. George Pipgras
   d. Johnny Broaca

5. Johnny Allen won 17 games for the Yankees as a rookie in 1932. For what team was he a 20-game winner later in his career?

6. Which of these pitchers was *not* a member of the starting rotation for the 1996 World Series champion Yankees?
   a. Dwight Gooden
   b. Jimmy Key
   c. Kenny Rogers
   d. David Wells

7. Which Boston pitcher served up Bucky Dent's home run in the 1978 Yankees-Red Sox one-game playoff? (Hint: This pitcher had been a member of the Yankees in 1977.)

8. Which member of the Yankees pitching staff did *not* get credited with a win in the 2009 World Series?
   a. Joba Chamberlain
   b. CC Sabathia
   c. A.J. Burnett
   d. Andy Pettitte

9. Who had a lower ERA as a Yankee: Red Ruffing or Lefty Gomez?

10. Ron Guidry won 25 games in 1978. Which other Yankees pitcher won 20 games that year?

Ten

Yankees Superstars

Here are ten questions each about the careers of eight of the greatest players in Yankees history.

The Babe puts another one in the seats.

Babe Ruth

1. In how many World Series did Babe Ruth appear?
2. How many World Series home runs did Ruth hit in his career?
3. For what team did Ruth play after he left the Yankees?
4. Who was the manager of the team with which the Babe finished his career?
5. Who was the pitcher when Ruth supposedly called his home run in the 1932 World Series?
6. During Ruth's career with the Yankees (1920 to 1934) four other players won the American League home run title. Who are they?
7. Babe Ruth (then with the Red Sox) and Tilly Walker of the Athletics shared the 1918 home run crown with 11. Who was the ALer who won the two previous HR titles with 9 in 1917 and 12 in 1916?
8. True or False? Babe Ruth was undefeated as a pitcher for the Yankees.
9. True or False? Ruth was undefeated in the World Series as a pitcher for the Red Sox.
10. Which former big leaguer managed Ruth when he was a pitcher for the Baltimore Orioles and then sold him to the Red Sox?

Answers

1. 10
2. 15
3. The Boston Braves
4. Bill McKechnie
5. Charlie Root of the Chicago Cubs
6. Ken Williams (1922, 39 HRs); Bob Meusel (1925, 33 HRs); Lou Gehrig (1931, 46, shared title with Ruth, and Gehrig won outright in 1934, with 49 HRs); Jimmie Foxx (1932, 58 HRs and 1933 with 48 HRs)
7. Wally Pipp of the Yankees
8. True, he was 5–0
9. True, he was 3–0
10. Jack Dunn

Lou Gehrig

1. Who portrayed Lou Gehrig in the movie *Pride of the Yankees*?
   a. Cary Grant
   b. James Stewart
   c. Clark Gable
   d. Gary Cooper

2. Gehrig won the AL MVP award in 1936. The next four highest vote getters that year are all in the Hall of Fame. Who were they?

3. Three other Hall of Famers received MVP votes in 1936. Who were they?

4. True or False? Lou Gehrig never struck out as many as 100 times in a season.

5. In what year did Gehrig win the Triple Crown?

6. How many times did Gehrig have 150 RBIs or more?

7. Did Babe Ruth have a greater or fewer number of 150 RBI seasons than Gehrig?

8. Only five players have a career OBP greater than .400 as members of the Yankees. The first three are Ruth, Gehrig, and Mantle. Who are the other two?

9. Gehrig has the most career triples as a Yankee with 163. Who is second on the Yankees career triples list?

10. Babe Ruth was one of four of Gehrig's teammates to play themselves in *Pride of the Yankees*. Who were the other three?

Joe DiMaggio

1. Which Indians third baseman made two spectacular plays to help end Joe DiMaggio's 56-game hitting streak on July 17, 1941?

2. Name the two hitters who finished the 1941 season with higher batting averages than DiMaggio, who hit .357.

3. Who was the only other Yankees starter to hit over .300 that season?

4. Who was the Giants pitcher in Game 6 of the 1951 World Series when Joe DiMaggio batted for the last time in his career? (Bonus: What did DiMaggio do in that last at-bat?)

5. Which four Hall of Fame pitchers gave up hits to DiMaggio during his 56-game hitting streak in 1941?

6. Joe's older brother, Vince, had his best year in 1942 (21 HR, 100 RBIs, .267 BA) as a member of which National League team?

7. In which hitting category did Vince DiMaggio lead the National League six times?

8. In which three seasons was Joe DiMaggio named the American League's Most Valuable Player?

9. Who was the National League MVP in the three seasons DiMaggio won the award in the AL?

10. What was the highest single-season strikeout total of Joe DiMaggio's career?

Answers

1. Ken Keltner
2. Ted Williams hit .406 (the last to hit over .400) and Cecil Travis of the Senators hit .359.
3. Phil Rizzuto (.307)
4. Larry Jansen (DiMaggio doubled to right field)
5. Lefty Grove, Bob Feller, Hal Newhouser, and Ted Lyons
6. Pittsburgh Pirates
7. Strikeouts
8. 1939, '41, and '47
9. Bucky Walters, '39 (Reds); Dolph Camilli, '41 (Dodgers); and Bob Elliott, '47 (Braves)
10. He struck out 39 times in 1936, his rookie year. Amazingly, DiMaggio struck out only 369 times in his career.

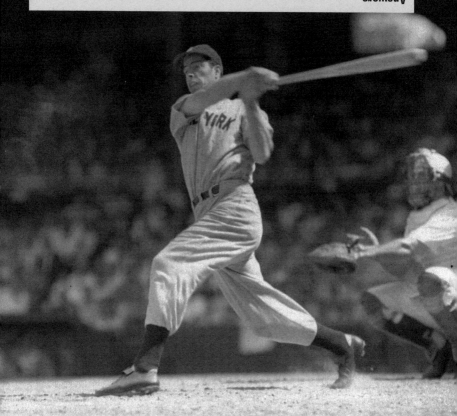

The sweet swing of the Yankee Clipper. Here DiMaggio hits in his 42nd straight game, breaking George Sisler's record of 41. The streak would increase to 56 games before coming to an end.

 **Quiz!**

Mickey Mantle

1. How many World Series home runs did Mantle hit in his career?
2. Which two Hall of Fame pitchers did Mickey hit World Series home runs off of?
3. Which two Hall of Fame pitchers did Mickey hit All-Star Game home runs off of?
4. How many times did Mantle hit home runs from both the left and right side in one game?
5. In what year did Mantle win the Triple Crown with 52 home runs, 130 RBIs, and a .353 BA?
6. As of the end of the 2010 season, five Yankees have 1,000 career walks. Mickey Mantle is second in career walks as a Yankee, with 1,733. Babe Ruth is first and Lou Gehrig is third. Name the other two Yankees who walked at least 1,000 times in their Yankees careers.
7. How many times did Mantle hit at least 40 home runs in a season?
8. Other than Yankee Stadium, in which AL ballpark did Mantle hit the most home runs?
9. Against which pitcher did Mickey Mantle hit the most regular-season home runs in his career?
10. How many grand slams did Mantle hit in his career?

Answers
1. 18
2. Sandy Koufax (1963) and Bob Gibson (1964)
3. Robin Roberts (1955) and Warren Spahn (1955)
4. 10 times
5. 1956
6. Bernie Williams (1,069) and Willie Randolph (1,005) are the other two. Going into the 2011 season, however, Derek Jeter had 948 walks.
7. Four times (1956, '58, '60, and '61)
8. Briggs Stadium/Tigers Stadium (42)
9. Early Wynn, with 13
10. Nine

 **Quiz!**

Reggie Jackson

1. What college did Reggie Jackson play for before his major league career?
2. Reggie's No. 44 has been retired by the Yankees. The Oakland A's also retired the number Jackson wore when he played for them. What is that number?
3. As a member of the A's, Jackson won the 1973 World Series MVP against which NL team?
4. As a Yankee, he won the 1977 World Series MVP against which NL team?
5. In Game 6 of the 1977 World Series Jackson hit three home runs off three separate pitchers. Who were they?
6. Which Yankees manager sparked a physical confrontation with Jackson in the dugout in Boston after he removed Jackson from the game for not hustling?
7. Which Hall of Fame pitcher was Jackson's teammate on both the A's and the Yankees?
8. In 1980, Jackson hit 41 home runs to share the AL homer title with which Brewers outfielder?
9. Reggie Jackson hit his 500th career home run against which Royals pitcher? (Hint: He later became a major league manager.)
10. In 1973, as a member of the A's, Jackson was voted as the AL MVP. The closest he ever got to another MVP award after that was a second-place finish. In what year and for what team?

Dave Winfield

1. Dave Winfield was a member of the varsity basketball team at which Big Ten school?
2. Which NFL team drafted him to play professional football?
3. For which NL team did Winfield begin his major league career?
4. His original team retired Winfield's number. What was that number?
5. How many Gold Gloves did Winfield win?
6. Which ESPN program does Dave Winfield co-host?
7. Dave Winfield was elected to how many consecutive All-Star Games?
8. With which four AL teams did Winfield play after leaving the Yankees?
9. Which Yankees teammate edged Winfield to win the 1984 AL batting title?
10. Off which Braves pitcher did Winfield hit a game-winning, two-run double in the 11ᵗʰ inning of Game 6 of the 1992 World Series?

Answers
1. Minnesota
2. Minnesota Vikings
3. San Diego Padres
4. 31
5. Seven
6. *Baseball Tonight*
7. 12, from 1977 to 1988
8. Angels, Blue Jays, Twins, and Indians
9. Don Mattingly (.343 to .340)
10. Charlie Leibrandt

Derek Jeter

1. How many times—prior to 2011—has Derek Jeter been elected to the AL All-Star squad?

2. Which Hall of Fame member was Jeter's childhood baseball hero?

3. Who was the runner Jeter cut down at the plate in his famous "flip" in Game 3 of the 2001 AL Division Series against the A's?

4. As of early 2011, Jeter was tied for fifth place with Bill Dickey and Wade Boggs in career batting average for the Yankees with a .313 average. Who are the top four Yankees of all time in this category?

5. Which old-time Yankees outfielder is immediately behind Jeter on the list at .311?

6. Name three of the four Yankees second basemen before Robinson Cano who were starters for the Yankees during Jeter's tenure at shortstop.

7. In 2000, Jeter became the only player in major league history to win which two awards in the same year?

8. Prior to 2011, what was the year (or years) that the Yankees failed to make it to the playoffs during Jeter's tenure as the starting shortstop?

9. How many times has Jeter finished in the top 10 in the AL MVP balloting?

10. Who was the AL MVP in 2006, the year that Jeter finished second?

Answers

1. 11
2. Dave Winfield
3. Jeremy Giambi
4. Babe Ruth (.349), Lou Gehrig (.340), Earle Combs (.325), and Joe DiMaggio (.325)
5. Bob Meusel
6. Mariano Duncan, Luis Sojo, Chuck Knoblauch, and Alfonso Soriano
7. He was named the MVP in both the All-Star Game and the World Series.
8. 2008
9. Seven
10. Justin Morneau of the Twins

Alex Rodriguez

1. For what teams and in what years did Rodriguez hit more than 50 home runs in a season?

2. Going into the 2011 season, Rodriguez was sixth on the all-time home run list with 613. Which five sluggers were ahead of him on the list?

3. Who are the two other Yankees who are in the top 20 in career HRs?

4. Going into the 2011 season, A-Rod ranked 20th in most career runs scored. Who are the only two people ahead of him who aren't in the Hall of Fame?

5. Who was the Yankees third basemen in 2002 and parts of 2003, before the team acquired A-Rod? (Bonus: Who started at third base to close out the 2003 season?)

6. Which players succeeded Rodriguez as their club's starting shortstop when he left the Seattle Mariners in 2001 and the Texas Rangers in 2004?

7. What team did A-Rod root for when he was growing up?

8. In 1996, Rodriguez won the AL batting crown with a .358 average, becoming the third-youngest player to win this award, at 21 years and 30 days. Which two former batting champions accomplished this feat at a younger age?

9. Who are the only four players in history besides A-Rod to win the MVP with two different teams?

10. Which pitcher served up A-Rod's 600th home run?

Eleven

The Match Game

Match the Yankees great with the city in which he grew up.

1. Derek Jeter   A. Milwaukee
2. Whitey Ford   B. Tampa
3. Joe DiMaggio   C. Chicago
4. Tino Martinez   D. Kansas City
5. Alex Rodriguez   E. Kalamazoo
6. Babe Ruth   F. St. Paul
7. Bill Skowron   G. Baltimore
8. Tony Kubek   H. New York
9. Dave Winfield   I. San Francisco
10. Casey Stengel   J. Miami

Match the Yankees Pitcher with the year he was a 20-game winner.

1.	Ron Guidry	A.	1996
2.	Vic Raschi	B.	1921
3.	Andy Pettitte	C.	1904
4.	Russ Ford	D.	1943
5.	Lefty Gomez	E.	1985
6.	Mel Stottlemyre	F.	2008
7.	Jack Chesbro	G.	1950
8.	Mike Mussina	H.	1934
9.	Carl Mays	I.	1911
10.	Spud Chandler	J.	1968

Match the pitcher to his primary catcher.

1.	Ed Lopat	A.	Thurman Munson
2.	Atley Donald	B.	Aaron Robinson
3.	Jim Bouton	C.	Jorge Posada
4.	Ed Figueroa	D.	Red Kleinow
5.	Urban Shocker	E.	Bill Dickey
6.	Jimmy Key	F.	Wally Schang
7.	Bullet Joe Bush	G.	Yogi Berra
8.	Bill Bevans	H.	Pat Collins
9.	Jack Chesbro	I.	Elston Howard
10.	David Wells	J.	Mike Stanley

Match the team with the year they were defeated by the Yankees in the World Series.

1.	Giants	A.	1943
2.	Mets	B.	1927
3.	Phillies	C.	1977
4.	Pirates	D.	1936
5.	Padres	E.	1998
6.	Cubs	F.	1961
7.	Braves	G.	2000
8.	Cardinals	H.	1932
9.	Reds	I.	2009
10.	Dodgers	J.	1999

Reggie Jackson connects on the second of his three home runs in Game 6 of the 1977 World Series.

Twelve

Yankees Honors and Awards

New York Yankees Elected to the National Baseball Hall of Fame
Catcher: Bill Dickey and Yogi Berra
First Base: Lou Gehrig and Johnny Mize
Second Base: Tony Lazzeri and Joe Gordon
Shortstop: Phil Rizzuto
Third Base: Frank "Home Run" Baker, Wade Boggs, and Joe Sewell
Outfield: Babe Ruth, Joe DiMaggio, Mickey Mantle, Dave Winfield, Earle Combs, "Wee Willie" Keeler, Rickey Henderson, Reggie Jackson, Enos Slaughter, and Paul Waner
Pitcher: Whitey Ford, Herb Pennock, Red Ruffing, Lefty Gomez, Goose Gossage, Waite Hoyt, Jack Chesbro, Stan Coveleski, Jim "Catfish" Hunter, Dazzy Vance, Gaylord Perry, Burleigh Grimes, and Phil Niekro
Yankees Managers: Miller Huggins, Joe McCarthy, and Casey Stengel
General Managers: Ed Barrow and George Weiss

Yankees Retired Numbers (and the year they were retired)
1 — Billy Martin (1986)
3 — Babe Ruth (1948)

4 — Lou Gehrig (1939)
5 — Joe DiMaggio (1952)
7 — Mickey Mantle (1969)
8 — Yogi Berra and Bill Dickey (1972)
9 — Roger Maris (1984)
10 — Phil Rizzuto (1985)
15 — Thurman Munson (1979)
16 — Whitey Ford (1974)
23 — Don Mattingly (1997)
32 — Elston Howard (1984)
37 — Casey Stengel (1970)
44 — Reggie Jackson (1993)
49 — Ron Guidry (2003)

Monument Park at Yankee Stadium

Since 1932 the Yankees have honored their all-time greats with
the dedication of monuments and plaques in Yankee Stadium.
The tradition continues in the current stadium in Monument Park,
located behind the center-field fence. The number in parentheses is
the year the monument or plaque was dedicated

Monuments
Miller Huggins (1932)
Lou Gehrig (1941)
Babe Ruth (1949)
Mickey Mantle (1996)*
Joe DiMaggio (1999)*
George Steinbrenner (2010)
*Mantle's and DiMaggio's plaques were dedicated in 1969

Plaques
Jacob Ruppert (Owner, 1940)

Ed Barrow (1954)
Joe McCarthy (1976)
Casey Stengel (1976)
Thurman Munson (1980)
Elston Howard (1984)
Roger Maris (1984)
Phil Rizzuto (1985)
Billy Martin (1986)
Lefty Gomez (1987)
Whitey Ford (1987)
Bill Dickey (1988)
Yogi Berra (1988)
Allie Reynolds (1989)
Don Mattingly (1997)
Mel Allen (Announcer, 1998)
Bob Sheppard (Public address announcer, 2000)
Reggie Jackson (2002)
Ron Guidry (2003)
Red Ruffing (2004)
Jackie Robinson (2007)

Other members and honorees

The Knights of Columbus donated plaques in honor of the Masses celebrated at Yankee Stadium by Pope Paul VI (1965), Pope John Paul II (1979), and Pope Benedict XVI (2008).

The Yankees dedicated a monument to the victims and rescue workers of 9/11 on September 11, 2002, the first anniversary of the attacks.

Prime 9

Prime 9 is a countdown show by MLB Productions for the MLB Network ranking the all-time top nine in a variety of categories.

Prime 9 is designed to start arguments, not end them. Here is a list of Yankees or bits of Yankees history that made the top nine on various shows and where they were ranked.

"Top 9 Rotations"
No. 5: 1927 Yankees—Waite Hoyt, Herb Pennock, Urban Shocker, Dutch Ruether, and George Pipgras

"Top 9 Double Play Combos"
No. 4: Phil Rizzuto and Joe Gordon

"Top 9 Greatest Infields"
No. 3: 2009 Yankees—Mark Teixeira, Robinson Cano, Derek Jeter, and Alex Rodriguez

"Top 9 Third Basemen"
No. 5: Wade Boggs
No. 9: Frank "Home Run" Baker

"Top 9 Best Sliders"
No. 2: Ron Guidry
No. 4: Sparky Lyle

"Top 9 Plays at the Plate"
No. 4: Derek Jeter flip
No. 6: Carlton Fisk tags out two Yankees (Bobby Meacham and Dale Berra).

"Top 9—All 1970s Team"
No. 9: Reggie Jackson, right field

"Top 9 Greatest Comebacks"
No. 1: 2004 Red Sox come back from 3–0 against the Yankees to win AL pennant.
No. 2: 1978 Yankees come back from 14 games down to force a one-game playoff with the Red Sox.

"Top 9 Baseball Gaffes"
No. 5: Mickey Owen's passed ball in Game 4 of the 1941 World Series that led to a Yankees rally and a victory in the game, leading to a 4–1 series win over the Dodgers
No. 9: Chuck Knoblauch arguing with the umpire in the 12th inning of Game 3 of the 1998 ALCS, which allowed the winning run to score from first base

"Top 9 Greatest Pitching Seasons"
No. 8: Ron Guidry, 1978

"Top 9 Greatest Rookie Seasons"
No. 7: Joe DiMaggio, 1936

"Top 9 Center Fielders"
No. 3: Mickey Mantle
No. 5: Joe DiMaggio

"Top 9 Unbreakable Records"
No. 3: Yankees five straight World Series titles
No. 4: Rickey Henderson, 1,406 steals
No. 8: Joe DiMaggio's 56-game hitting streak

"Top 9 Home Runs"
No. 6: Babe Ruth's called shot in the 1932 World Series
No. 8: Aaron Boone in the 2003 ALCS
No. 9: Chris Chambliss in the 1976 ALCS

"Top 9 Shortstops"
No. 6: Derek Jeter

"Top 9 Clutch Hitters"
No. 1: Babe Ruth
No. 2: Reggie Jackson
No. 3: Lou Gehrig
No. 6: Derek Jeter

"Top 9 Closers"
No. 1: Mariano Rivera
No. 6: Goose Gossage

"Top 9 Catchers"
No. 1: Yogi Berra
No. 2: Bill Dickey

"Top 9 Managers"
No. 2: Joe McCarthy
No. 3: Casey Stengel
No. 9: Joe Torre

"Top 9 Outfield Arms"
No. 2: Jesse Barfield

"Top 9 Trades"
No. 1: Babe Ruth from the Red Sox for $125,000

"Top 9 Left Fielders"
No. 4: Rickey Henderson

"Top 9 Designated Hitters"
No. 7: Don Baylor
No. 8: Chili Davis

"Top 9 Players of the '80s"
First Base: Don Mattingly
Left Field: Rickey Henderson

"Top 9 Team Broadcasters"
No. 2: Mel Allen
No. 3: Red Barber
No. 8: Phil Rizzuto
No. 9: Curt Gowdy

"Top 9 Greatest Ballparks"
No. 1: Old Yankee Stadium

Yankees Awards

Most Valuable Player

2007 — Alex Rodriguez
2005 — Alex Rodriguez
1985 — Don Mattingly
1976 — Thurman Munson
1963 — Elston Howard
1962 — Mickey Mantle
1961 — Roger Maris
1957 — Mickey Mantle
1956 — Mickey Mantle
1955 — Yogi Berra
1954 — Yogi Berra
1951 — Yogi Berra
1950 — Phil Rizzuto
1947 — Joe DiMaggio
1943 — Spud Chandler
1942 — Joe Gordon
1941 — Joe DiMaggio
1939 — Joe DiMaggio
1936 — Lou Gehrig
1927 — Lou Gehrig
1923 — Babe Ruth

Rookie of the Year

1996 — Derek Jeter
1981 — Dave Righetti
1970 — Thurman Munson
1968 — Stan Bahnsen
1962 — Tom Tresh
1957 — Tony Kubek

1954 — Bob Grim
1951 — Gil McDougald

Batting
Triple Crown
Lou Gehrig, 1934: 49 HR, 165 RBI, .363 BA
Mickey Mantle, 1956: 52 HR, 130 RBI, .353 BA

Silver Slugger Award
First Base: Don Mattingly, (3) 1985, '86, and '87; Jason Giambi, 2002; Tino Martinez, 1997
Second Base: Robinson Cano, (2) 2006 and '10; Willie Randolph, 1980; Alfonso Soriano, 2002
Shortstop: Derek Jeter, (4) 2006–09
Third Base: Alex Rodriguez, (3) 2005, '07, and '08; Wade Boggs, (2) 1993–94
Outfield: Dave Winfield, (4) 1981–82, '84–85; Gary Sheffield, (2) 2004–05; Rickey Henderson, 1985; Bernie Williams, 2002
Catcher: Jorge Posada, (5) 2000–03, and '07; Mike Stanley, 1993
Designated Hitter: Don Baylor, (2) 1983 and '85; Reggie Jackson, 1980

Hitting for the Cycle
Bob Meusel, (3) 1921, '22, and '28
Joe DiMaggio, (2) 1937 and 1948
Lou Gehrig, (2) 1934
Tony Lazzeri, 1932 (natural order—single, double, triple, grand slam)
Tony Fernandez, 1995
Bert Daniels, 1912
Melky Cabrera, 2009
Joe Gordon, 1940

Mickey Mantle, 1957
Bobby Murcer, 1972
Buddy Rosar, 1940

Fielding
Gold Glove
First Base: Don Mattingly, (9) 1985–89, 1991–94; Joe Pepitone, (3)
1965–66, and '69; Mark Teixeira, (2) 2009–10; Chris Chambliss, 1978
Second Base: Bobby Richardson, (5) 1961–65; Robinson Cano, 2010
Shortstop: Derek Jeter, (5) 2004–06, 2009–10
Third Base: Graig Nettles, (2) 1977–78; Wade Boggs, (2) 1994–95;
Scott Brosius, 1999
Outfield: Bernie Williams, (4) 1997–00; Dave Winfield, (4) 1982–85;
Mickey Mantle, 1962; Roger Maris, 1960; Bobby Murcer, 1972; Norm
Siebern, 1958; Tom Tresh, 1965
Catcher: Thurman Munson, (3) 1973–75; Elston Howard, (2) 1963–64
Pitcher: Ron Guidry, (5) 1982–86; Bobby Shantz, (4) 1957–60; Mike
Mussina, (3) 2001–03

Pitching
Cy Young Award
Roger Clemens, 2001
Ron Guidry, 1978
Sparky Lyle, 1977
Whitey Ford, 1961 for MLB
Bob Turley, 1958 for MLB

Pitching Triple Crown (ERA, Wins, and Strikeouts)
Lefty Gomez, 1934: 2.33 ERA, 26 Wins, 158 SO
Lefty Gomez, 1937: 2.33 ERA, 21 Wins, 194 SO

Fireman or Reliever of the Year
Luis Arroyo, 1961
Sparky Lyle, 1972
Rich "Goose" Gossage, 1978
Dave Righetti, (2) 1986 and 1987 (shared with Jeff Reardon of the Twins)
John Wetteland, 1996
Mariano Rivera, (6) 1997, '99, '01, '04–05, and '09 (shared with Joe Nathan of the Twins)

Manager of the Year
Joe Torre, (2) 1996 (shared with Johnny Oates of the Rangers) and '98
Buck Showalter, 1994

Thirteen

Yankee-isms

There were three characters on those New York Yankees teams of the early '50s who are still being quoted today, more than a half century later, and will probably still be quoted a century from now.

Manager Casey Stengel was famous during his playing and managerial career as an imp and a character with many stories attesting to his wit and clownishness. As a manager, he entertained writers, fellow baseball people, and the public with his wry observations and his new language. "Stengelese" was a long, meandering method of answering questions and telling stories that bordered on double-talk, but according to those who knew him, "he always had a point." While he was famous for Stengelese, he didn't get as much attention when he managed the great Yankees teams as he would later in his career when he managed the hapless Mets. There he would use his brand of humor as a distraction, in an attempt to grab attention away from the ineptitude on the field.

Yogi Berra's "Yogi-isms" weren't meant to be humorous, they were merely observations and replies by a man who didn't have great command of the nuances of the language. What he had was a sound lifeview and philosophy, but he expressed it in a colorful, slightly askew, manner. Most of the famous Yogi quotes had a certain logic to them if you really read or listened to them. Many "Yogi-isms" have become part of the American lexicon.

Jerry Coleman was a Yankees All-Star second baseman who played on four of the Bombers world championship teams. He was also a decorated war hero as a marine aviator who flew numerous combat missions, serving in both World War II and Korea. He rose to the rank of Lieutenant Colonel.

When Coleman's playing days were over he joined the Yankees broadcasting team for seven years and then joined San Diego, where he celebrated his 39th season as the voice of the Padres in 2011. In 2005, the Hall of Fame awarded him with the Ford C. Frick award.

Coleman is also famous for his malaprops, slight misstatements that he uttered on the air that gave his intended point a whole new meaning.

Here they are, some of the best of "Stengelese," "Yogi-isms," and "Jerry Coleman-isms."

Stengelese

"They say some of my stars drink whiskey, but I have found that ones who drink milkshakes don't win many ballgames."

"Being with a woman all night never hurt no professional baseball player. It's staying up all night looking for a woman that does him in."

"You gotta learn that if you don't get it by midnight, chances are you ain't gonna get it, and if you do, it ain't worth it."

"Good pitching will always stop good hitting and vice versa."

"Son, we'd like to keep you around this season, but we're going to try and win a pennant."

"You have to have a catcher because if you don't you're likely to have a lot of passed balls."

"I don't know if he throws a spitball, but he sure spits on the ball."

"There comes a time in every man's life, and I've had plenty of them."

"They say Yogi Berra is funny. Well, he has a lovely wife and family, a beautiful home, money in the bank, and he plays golf with millionaires. What's funny about that?"

"Without losers, where would the winners be?"

"Most ballgames are lost, not won."

"It's wonderful to meet so many friends that I didn't used to like."

"Now there's three things you can do in a baseball game: you can win or you can lose or it can rain."

"He's only 20 years old and with a good chance in 10 years of being 30."—about one of his Mets "prospects"

"Don't cut my throat. I may want to do that later, myself."

"I was such a dangerous hitter I even got intentional walks during batting practice."

"The key to being a good manager is keeping the five guys who hate me away from the five who are still undecided."

"Don't drink in the hotel bar, that's where I do my drinking."—Stengel's instruction to his players.

"If anyone wants me, tell them I'm being embalmed."

"Can't anybody here play this game?"—Casey about his original Mets.

"I got players with bad watches—they can't tell midnight from noon."

"Never make predictions, especially about the future."

"I've been in the game 100 years, but the Mets have shown me more ways to lose than I ever knew existed."

"All right everyone, line up alphabetically according to your height."

"I don't like them fellas who drive in two runs and let in three."

"Two hundred million Americans, and there ain't two good catchers among 'em"

"When you are younger you get blamed for crimes you never committed and when you're older you begin to get credit for virtues you never possessed. It evens itself out."

"We [the Mets] are a much improved ball club, now we lose in extra innings."

On how it feels to be 75 years old: "Most people my age are dead at the present time."

"He's a remarkable catcher, that Canzoneri [Mets catcher Chris Cannizzaro]. He's the only catcher in baseball who can't catch."

On being fired as manager of the Yankees: "They told me my services were no longer desired, because they wanted to put in a youth program as an advance way of keeping the club going. I'll never make the mistake of being 70 again."

And, the greatest example of "Stengelese" ever, Casey Stengel's famous testimony to Congress when questioned about the antitrust issue:

"I would say I would not know, but would say the reason why they would want it passed is to keep baseball going as the highest paid ball sport that has gone into baseball and from the baseball angle, I am not going to speak of any other sport. I am not here to argue about other sports, I am in the baseball business. It has been run cleaner than any business that was ever put out in the 100 years at the present time. I am not speaking about television or I am not speaking about income that comes into the ballparks: you have to take that off. I don't know too much about it. I say the ballplayers have a better advancement at the present time."

And then Mickey Mantle, who was the next to testify, simply stated, "My views are about the same as Casey's."

Yogi-isms

"It ain't over, 'til it's over."

"It's like déjà vu all over again."

"Nobody goes there anymore, because it's too crowded."

"Ninety percent of this game is half mental."

"When you get to a fork in the road, take it."

"I didn't really say everything I said."

"The future ain't what it used to be."

"A nickel ain't worth a dime anymore."

When he was told by the wife of the mayor of New York that he looked cool in his summer suit, Yogi said, "Thank you. You don't look so hot yourself."

When he was ordering pizza, Yogi was asked how many slices he would like his pizza cut into, he answered, "You better make it four. I don't think I could eat eight."

"It gets late early around here."

"If you don't know where you're going, you'll wind up somewhere else."

"Our similarities are different."

"I want to thank you for making this day necessary."

When asked the time, Yogi answered, "What? Do you mean right now?"

"Never answer an anonymous letter."

"Slump? I ain't in no slump...I just ain't hitting."

"You can observe a lot by watching."

"If I didn't wake up I'd still be sleeping."

"We have a good time together, even when we're not together."

"I usually take a two-hour nap, from one to four."

"If they don't want to come, you can't stop them."

"Think? How the hell are you gonna think and hit at the same time?"

"Why buy good luggage? You only use it when you travel."

When his wife Carmen asked where he would like to be buried, Yogi said, "Surprise me!"

"Always go to other people's funerals, otherwise they won't go to yours."

Jerry Coleman-isms

"Dave Winfield goes back to the wall, he hits his head on the wall and it rolls off! It's rolling all the way back to second base. This is a terrible thing for the Padres."

"There's someone warming up in the bullpen, but he's obscured by his number."

"Rich Folkers is throwing up in the bullpen."

"McCovey swings and misses. It's fouled back."

"Templeton is as hot as you can be and still walk."

"That home run ties it up 1–0."

"Ozzie makes a leaping, diving stop, shovels to Fernando and everybody drops everything."

"(Johnny) Grubb goes back, back. He's under the warning track."

"Graig Nettles leaped up to make one of those diving stops only he can make."

"Ozzie Smith just made another play that I've never seen anyone else make before, and I've seen him make it more often than anyone else ever has."

"The first pitch to Tucker Ashford is grounded into left field—no, wait a minute. It's ball 1, low and outside."

"That's Hendrick's 19th home run. One more and he reaches double figures."

"George Hendrick simply lost that sun-blown pop-up."

"On the mound is Randy Jones, the left-hander with the Karl Marx hairdo."

"Larry Moffett is 6' 3". Last year he was 6' 6"."

"Eric Show will be oh-for-ten if that pop fly comes down."

"I've made a couple of mistakes I'd like to do over."

"Young Frank Pastore may have just pitched the biggest victory of 1979, maybe the biggest victory of the year."

"Those amateur umpires are certainly flexing their fangs tonight."

"Gaylord Perry and Willie McCovey should know each other like a book. They've been ex-teammates for years now."

"Johnny Grubb slides into second with a stand-up double."

"Mike Caldwell, the Padres' right-handed southpaw, will pitch tonight."

Fourteen

Yankees All-Star Teams

This chapter includes five New York Yankees All-Star teams, just for fun. In this league the players can show up for more than one team. (Gehrig and Whitey are both on three teams, and their teammates are happy to have them.) As always, we apologize if we've omitted anyone significant from any category.

The All-Yankees Manager Team

We would call this team solid, but without much pitching depth, though Lemon gives you a Hall of Famer at the top of the rotation. We do need a closer, though. Yogi, Dickey, and Torre would anchor the lineup. Chase and Chance, a pair of deadball-era guys, would fight it out at first base. The middle infield is just fair. In the outfield, Yogi and Casey could hit—and say amusing things—and Virdon is a great middleman. Piniella as DH would be important to the lineup.

First Base: Hal Chase, Frank Chance

Second Base: Billy Martin, Bucky Harris, Miller Huggins

Shortstop: Roger Peckinpaugh, Bucky Dent, Gene Michael, Dick Howser, Kid Elberfeld

Third Base: Joe Torre, Harry Wolverton

George Steinbrenner hugs Billy Martin after the Yankees defeated the Kansas City Royals in the 1977 ALCS to advance to the World Series.

Left Field: Yogi Berra
Center Field: Bill Virdon
Right Field: Casey Stengel
Catcher: Bill Dickey, Joe Girardi
Designated Hitter: Lou Piniella
Pitcher: Bob Lemon, Bob Shawkey, Clark Griffith, "Wild Bill" Donovan, Clyde King, Dallas Green

The All-Broadcasters Team

The announcing careers of Ford and Mantle were short, but they do give this team a strong nucleus. White is one of the most underrated first basemen of all time (as is Tino, who is our lefty DH). Second base is shared, as it was in the early and mid-'50s, by a pair of solid players, and Scooter is a Hall of Famer at short.

Kubek would have to move to third (Martin could fill in), but that's okay, he's played it before. The outfield is one of the team's great strengths. And Piniella is a solid righty to add depth to the lineup. McCarver is one of the better catchers of the second half of the 20th century. And, as it does for all of these teams, the pitching staff needs relievers. But a starting rotation that can throw Diz, Seaver, and Whitey can probably take you a long way. Cone, Kaat, John, and Leiter ain't chopped liver, either.

First Base: Bill White
Second Base: Jerry Coleman, Billy Martin
Shortstop: Phil Rizzuto
Third Base: Tony Kubek
Left Field: Ken Singleton
Center Field: Mickey Mantle, Bobby Murcer
Right Field: Paul O'Neill
Catcher: Tim McCarver, Fran Healy
Designated Hitter: Tino Martinez, Lou Piniella
Pitchers: Dizzy Dean, David Cone, Jim Kaat, Tommy John, Tom Seaver, Al Leiter, Whitey Ford

The All-Born-or-Raised-in-the-New York-Metropolitan-Area Team

These are the homegrown guys—and we're taking the liberty of including Jeter and A-Rod because it's our book. The starting infield of Gehrig, Randolph, Jeter, and A-Rod would be the best of all time. In the outfield there's some power in Colavito and some hitting where they ain't with Hall of Famer Keeler. Cerone and Rosar are capable catchers, nothing flashy. Murphy was a fine relief pitcher in his time, and he closes for a rotation that includes two Hall of Famers and a boatload of 20-game winners.

We've included players from New York and nearby suburban New Jersey. We're giving everyone in Connecticut to the Red Sox and those from South Jersey to the Phillies.

If you think about it, though, the presence of Jeter and Rodriguez really makes this team.

First Base: Lou Gehrig, Joe Collins

Second Base: Willie Randolph, George Stirnweiss

Shortstop: Derek Jeter (born in Pequannock, NJ, raised in Kalamazoo, MI), Phil Rizzuto

Third Base: Alex Rodriguez (born in New York, NY, raised in Miami, FL), Dale Berra, Billy Johnson

Left Field: Lee Mazzilli, Elliott Maddox

Center Field: Joe Pepitone

Right Field: Rocky Colavito, "Wee Willie" Keeler

Catcher: Rick Cerone, Buddy Rosar

Designated Hitter: Dan Pasqua

Pitchers: Whitey Ford, Waite Hoyt, Ed Lopat, Jim Bouton, Hank Borowy, Bob Grim, Johnny Kucks, Johnny Murphy, Tom Ferrick, Tom Gorman, Pete Mikkelson

The All-Yankees Captain Team

First Base: Lou Gehrig

Second Base: Willie Randolph, Kid Elberfeld

Shortstop: Derek Jeter, Roger Peckinpaugh, Everett Scott

Third Base: Graig Nettles

Left Field: Hal Chase

Center Field: Don Mattingly

Right Field: Babe Ruth

Catcher: Thurman Munson

Designated Hitter: Frank Chance

Pitcher: Clark Griffith, Ron Guidry

The All-Time Yankees-for-Life Team

When the manager of this team finally made the roster cuts, we would take this group over any team you can come up with. It includes seven Hall of Famers, plus Jeter and Rivera, who are sure things. Admittedly, the pitching is a little thin. We'd have to find some major league set-up men for the bullpen. But a rotation that starts with Ford, Stottlemyre, and Guidry, and ends with Mo as the closer, should be enough with this lineup:

1. Jeter SS
2. Mattingly DH
3. Mantle CF
4. Gehrig 1B
5. DiMaggio RF
6. Cano 2B
7. Dickey C
8. B. Williams LF
9. Rolfe 3B

And that's not to mention the likes of Rizzuto, Munson, Henrich, and Combs coming off the bench. I guess this explains why the Yankees have dominated baseball for almost a century.

Here it is. A Yankees team comprised solely of players who played only for the Yankees in their major league careers:

First Base: Lou Gehrig, Don Mattingly, Joe Collins

Second Base: Gil McDougald, Jerry Coleman, Robinson Cano

Shortstop: Frank Crosetti, Phil Rizzuto, Tony Kubek, Derek Jeter

Third Base: Red Rolfe, Bobby Brown

Outfield: Joe DiMaggio, Earle Combs, George Selkirk, Tommy Henrich, Mickey Mantle, Roy White, Bernie Williams

Catcher: Bill Dickey, Thurman Munson, Jorge Posada

Pitcher: Spud Chandler, Atley Donald, Whitey Ford, Mel Stottlemyre, Ron Guidry, Mariano Rivera